The ABC'S of Canning and Preserving

Everything You Need to Know to Can Vegetables, Meals and Meats

Cassandra Williams

© Copyright 2020 - All Rights Reserved

The content within this book may not be reproduced, duplicated, or transmitted without direct written permission from the author or the publisher.

Under no circumstances will any blame or legal responsibility be held against the publisher, or author, for any damages, reparation or monetary loss due to the information contained within this book, either directly or indirectly.

Legal Notice

This book is copyright protected. This book is only for personal use. You cannot amend, distribute, sell, use, quote or paraphrase any part, or the content within this book, without the consent of the author or publisher.

Disclaimer Notice

Please note the information contained within this document is for educational and entertainment purposes only. All effort has been executed to present accurate, up-to-date and reliable, complete information. No warranties of any kind are declared or implied. Readers acknowledge that the author is not engaging in the rendering of legal, financial, medical or professional advice.

Table of Contents

- Introduction..3
- Simple Guide to Storing Fruits and Vegetables......................7
- Freezing Fruits and Vegetables...13
- How to Can Fruits and Vegetables..26
- Drying Fruits and Vegetables 56
- Pickling Fruits & Vegetables..69
- Making Jams and Jellies 84
- Making Chutneys 121
- Vegetable Soups 134
- Fruit Leathers...144
- Fruit Butters & Cheeses..149
- Fruit Curds..156
- Ketchups & Sauces...163
- Fruit Cordials & Syrups..171
- Conclusion...181

Introduction

Growing your own fruits and vegetables at home is very rewarding, but the issue most people face is that they harvest far more than they can use. A single courgette (zucchini) plant can produce a couple of dozen courgettes during the growing season, but it is very hard for even the most seasoned fan to use that many.

Although you can use succession planting to try to minimize the risk of a glut of produce, there still comes a time when you are overwhelmed by what you have grown and need to do something to store it, particularly if you have fruit trees or bushes.

Refrigerating your produce does work, but it provides a short-term storage solution when, ideally, you need to store your fresh produce for months instead of days or weeks. Before refrigeration people had solved this problem, but in our convenience society the knowledge of preserving foods are mostly forgotten by all except homesteaders and a few grandparents.

This book will talk you through the various methods of preserving fruits and vegetables, all of which works as well for shop bought produce as for home grown produce. You will learn a wide variety of preservation methods and which fruits and vegetables they are best for. These methods will allow you to store your fresh fruits and vegetables for months, if not a year or two in some cases.

Although many people cram their freezer or fridge full of food, what they don't know is that over time it loses flavor, appearance and nutritional value. Stored incorrectly, some fruits and vegetables become positively inedible when frozen for too long. However, this book will show you how to preserve even delicate fruits like strawberries for months. We will discuss freezing produce in this book too, but you will learn other methods that do not require electricity to store.

When storing your home-grown produce, you will be surprised how quickly you run out of space. When I was running three allotments I had four freezers and two refrigerators in my garage which I used to store everything I grew, not to mention everything that was hung from the roof or stored in bags. Even then, I still ran out space on occasion.

For me, one of the biggest benefits of preserving home-grown fruits and vegetables is that it is a huge money saver. Growing your own produce can be much cheaper than buying it in the shops, particularly if you are growing expensive, hard to get hold of plants. It means that during the winter months you have access to free home grown produce and healthy food. There is something quite special about enjoying home grown strawberries in the middle of winter ... they taste divine, far better than anything you can buy in the stores at that time.

One of the simplest ways of storing produce is to dry it and keep it somewhere cool and dry. This works well for onions and garlic.
Apples and beetroot can also be stored in similar conditions and, when stored correctly, will last for months. Some varieties of apples will last through to spring in the ideal conditions.

Canning is one of the best ways to store produce, which does require some work but allows produce to be stored for a good number of months. This method of preservation, although discovered by a French man (Nicolar Appert), is far more popular in the USA than it is across Europe. In this method, harmful micro- organisms are destroyed through a heating process and then the food is stored in an air-tight environment.

The real benefit of canning is that the nutritional value of the food is preserved, though some will be lost through heating as with any cooked food. The food will last for a long time and will taste as good as the day you canned it when you open it. Some people have kept their canned produce for years.

Storing your own produce is a great way of dealing with the glut of fruits and vegetables any home grower will often experience. You will learn lots of different ways to store your produce, including some rather cool modern methods, plus lots and lots of recipes and ideas of what to make with your vegetables.

Enjoy preserving your home-grown fruits and vegetables, and enjoy eating them even more!

Simple Guide to Storing Fruits and Vegetables

A lot of fresh fruits and vegetables can be stored outside of a refrigerator or freezer and without any processing. Some will last for a few weeks, whereas others will last for several months and a few, such as onions and garlic can last close to a year, when stored in ideal conditions. This is a great way for you to store fresh produce whilst you are waiting to use it. If you have a lot, then the other methods, detailed later, for long term storage are better to use. For shorter term storage of most fresh fruits and vegetables, this method is ideal.

In a minute, I'll detail some of the produce commonly grown and how they are best stored without any preservation methods being applied. After this chapter, we will talk about the many other ways that you can preserve fruits and vegetables that involve some processing and packaging.

Personally, I store some of my produce like this, usually the damaged stuff and use it over the following few weeks. The good quality produce, if it doesn't get used immediately, will get stored using one of the other methods later in this books for use over the year. Typically, all home-made products will be used within a year, with friends and family benefiting from it all. By the time you hit the next harvest time, you have used up most of your preserved produce, if not all of it, and are ready to start again.

You will need somewhere cool, dark and dry to store your produce. This could be a root cellar, a basement or a garage. You need good air circulation and a temperature of between 50-55F with low humidity. All fruits and vegetables should be stored so they are not touching each other. Do not wash any vegetable before storage.
Brush off any loose or excess dirt, trim the roots and any foliage. The moment you wash or clean your fruit and vegetables, then it will start to decompose and rot. This is why dirty potatoes store far better than the pretty washed ones we buy in the supermarkets ... my home-grown potatoes will store for several months, whereas the store-bought ones can struggle to last a few weeks.

When storing your fresh produce, you need to check them regularly, particularly cauliflower and broccoli as you can find slugs and other pests hide in them and you may not find them all (this is why I'm banned from putting vegetables from my allotment in the family fridge).

Beans – store in a single layer on shelves or a table. Lasts 2-4 weeks.

Beetroot – store in boxes filled with sand, not touching. Can last for 6 to 12 months.

Broccoli – store in a single layer on a shelf and it will last for 2 to 3 months. If refrigerating, wrap in plastic wrap to prevent it from going limp.

Brussels Sprouts – leave on the stalk in the ground, removing all leaves except those at the top where the Brussels sprouts will last through winter and into spring. You can harvest and store in a double layer on a shelf/table where they will last for 3 to 4 months.

Butternut Squash – store in bins or boxes and they will last for 6 to 9 months.

Cabbages – store in bins or baskets where they can last for 3 to 4 months.

Carrots – store in sand in boxes, not touching and they can last for 6 to 9 months.

Cauliflower – remove outer leaves, check for slugs and store on a shelf where they will last for 3 to 4 months.

Cucumbers – store in a double layer on a shelf. Will last for 4 to 6 weeks.

Sweet corn – remove silk from ends and any loose leaves, leaving the cob in the tightly wrapped leaves. Store on a shelf in a single layer where they will last a week or two.

Celery - store on a shelf in a single layer, removing loose or damaged leaves. Check thoroughly for slugs and snails. They will last for one or two weeks. It is better, if you can, to leave celery in the ground until you need it.

Eggplant (aubergine) – store in a single layer on a shelf where they will last for one to two weeks.

Leeks – remove excess leaves, check for slugs and snails. Tie the tops together in groups of 4 to 6 and hang, where they can last anything from 6 to 12 months. These can also be left in the ground until you need them in all but the coldest or wettest of areas.

Onions – remove excess dirt, trim roots and hang where they will store for around 9 months.

Parsnips – can be left in the ground over winter where the frost makes them sweeter. Store on a shelf in a single layer, brushing off excess dirt where they will last 6 to 9 months.

Peas – do not shell, store on a shelf where they will last for 2 or 3 weeks.

Potatoes – store in bins or hessian / paper sacks, brushing off excess dirt where they will last for 6 to 9 months. Main crop potatoes store the longest for up to nine months in ideal conditions. First early potatoes will only store for a couple of months.

Peppers – store, not touching, on a shelf where they will stay fresh for a week or two.

Sweet Potatoes – store in bins or hessian/paper sacks where they will last 6 to 9 months.

Tomatoes (ripe) – store on a shelf where they will last a week or two. Green tomatoes will last longer, up to a month or two and can be ripened with the usual methods.

Turnips – store in boxes or bags where they will last 6 to 9 months.

Fruits can be stored in a similar manner. Again, remove any damaged fruits to use first and check for pests. All fruits are best stored not touching each other, as that encourages rot.

Apples – store on shelves, not touching, or in bins surrounded by sand where they can last for up to nine months, depending on the variety – late apples store better than early ones.
Figs – store in a single layer and they will keep for up to a month.
Melons – store in a single layer, not touching and they will last from two to three weeks.
Pears – store on shelves, not touching and they will last for 3 to 4 weeks.

Some people will create a special root cellar to store their produce in, but for most of us that just isn't practical. For the majority of people, vegetables will be stored in the kitchen, in the cupboard under the stairs or in the garage. Unfortunately, in these less than ideal conditions, storage times are dramatically reduced, which is why so many people turn to other methods of preservation to store their food.

When you are storing your produce in bins or boxes they should be hand built so that they allow for air to circulate around the vegetables. Some people will use shallow wire baskets which allow for air circulation. Avoid plastic boxes as there is no ventilation, they encourage condensation and your hard work ends up rotting far too quickly. You can use normal shelves or construct some yourself specially for your vegetables, just make sure that the vegetables are not touching each other as that will encourage them to rot. You should also regularly check your produce when stored, turning it and making sure it hasn't started to rot.

A lot of people will take this approach to storing their produce:

Damaged produce is put in the refrigerator and used immediately
The best examples are shown off to friends and family, usually being used in a special meal
A portion of produce is stored normally, bearing in mind most people do not have a root cellar, and used over the next few weeks

The rest of the produce is preserved through drying, canning, freezing, pickling or making into something else

There is no right or wrong answer to how to store your produce. You need to store it in whatever way works for you and your family. Use whichever storage methods and recipes you like. As long as the fruits and vegetables are properly prepared before storing and then stored correctly, they can last for a year or more.

Now you know how to store your fresh produce "normally" it is time for you to learn some of the other methods of preserving your home- grown produce. Remember, this can be done for any store-bought produce, particularly when your favorites are in season and really cheap to buy!

Freezing Fruits and Vegetables

One of the most popular, and some would argue, the easiest, ways of storing your fresh fruits and vegetables is in your freezer. Almost everyone has a freezer at home and it is one way to store produce and keep it fresh for several months, if it is prepared properly first.

However, be aware that you may quickly fill your freezer and need to buy an additional one or use some of the other preservation methods discussed later, depending on how much you are trying to store.

It is best to freeze produce when it is perfectly ripe. Once it goes over-ripe then you can still freeze it, but it will not be the best quality. It's better to freeze over-ripe fresh produce rather than throw it away. All vegetables need to be blanched before freezing, then
plunged into ice water before being dried and put in the freezer. This is extremely important to kill bacteria and ensure the vegetables stay fresh whilst frozen.

You need to freeze produce as soon as possible after harvesting, ideally the same day. They must be stored in air-tight bags or containers and have as little air in as possible. Vacuum packing, which we will talk about soon, is the best way of scaling for long term freezing.

Fruits and vegetables with a high water content, e.g. Zucchini, cucumber, strawberries, melon and so on tend not to freeze as well as the freezing process causes cellular damage to the produce as the water molecules expand and damage the cell walls. Freezing high water content fruits and vegetables immediately and rapidly will produce smaller water crystals, which causes less damage to the cellular structure during freezing. Frozen fruit is often best eaten before it is completely thawed, while still slightly frozen as when it defrosts, the cellular structure tends to collapse as ice turns to water.

Most frozen fruits will store for up to a year, whereas vegetables can freeze for up to a year and a half. They will stay in the freezer for longer, but you can find the quality deteriorates the longer they are frozen. Using a vacuum sealer, and vacuum packing your fresh produce roughly doubles the freezing time before any damage occurs.

When freezing your produce, you should also label it with the name of what has been frozen and the date it was frozen on. This makes sure you can clearly identify what you are putting in the freezer. By

dating it, you know which frozen items need to be used first to prevent items being left in the freezer too long and going past their best.

How to Freeze Berries

Frozen fruit is fantastic because you can enjoy fruit from your garden throughout the year. One of my favorite recipes is to make an "ice cream" from frozen mixed berries and a thick, natural yoghurt. They are put in the blender until smooth and then eaten ... you ought to try it ... it's absolutely divine.

Depending on how you are planning on using your fruit there are three main ways to freeze fruit.

1)   Dry pack – this is best for smaller fruits that remain whole such as berries like blueberries or cranberries. Wash the fruit, dry it, then pack it into a container as tightly as possible without damaging the fruit. This works best if you pack a certain weight of fruit that you regularly use in recipes such as half or one pound per container. This allows you to take a specific weight of fruit out of the freezer at once as the fruit will all stick together and will not be easy to separate. A variation on this is a tray pack, where you spread the fruit out on a shallow tray (such as a baking tray), making sure they do not touch and then freeze. Once they are frozen you can easily pack them into bags or containers, label and freeze. The tray pack method generally allows you to remove as many berries as you need from the freezer rather than one large mass of berries as they do not freeze together into a lump.

2)   Sugar Pack – a lot of fruits will freeze well when packed with sugar. This can cause some fruit to darken, which can be

avoided by adding some lemon juice in water at a ratio of ½ teaspoon lemon juice to 3 tablespoons of water. Sprinkle this over the fruit and it will stop it from going brown, mixing the fruit up to ensure it is thoroughly covered. Leave it to stand for about 15 minutes before packaging up and freezing. This is ideal for fruits such as apricots, sliced apples, cherries (de- stoned), peaches, raspberries and strawberries.

3)	Syrup Pack – most fruits can be frozen preserved in syrup which is made by dissolving sugar in water. A medium syrup will be 1¾ cups of sugar to 4 cups of lukewarm water, stirring until all the sugar is dissolved. Chill the syrup before using it. Use just enough syrup to cover the fruit in its container, then place some parchment paper on top of the fruit before putting the lid on to keep the fruit under the syrup.

Any of these methods will work for storing your fresh fruit and it is a great way to preserve it for use during the winter months when many of the fruits you grow at home are expensive to buy from the stores and don't taste anywhere near as nice. Use whichever method you feel most comfortable with, depending on what type of fruit you are freezing.

How to Freeze Fresh Fruit

Freezing fresh fruits such as strawberries, blueberries, blackberries, apples, raspberries and so on is easy, but does need a bit of work on your part. You will need a baking sheet and some parchment paper, as well as some heavy duty freezer bags.

Firstly, sort through the fruit and remove any damaged fruit as it doesn't freeze well, so use it straight away. Rinse the fruit under cold running water, then lay it out on a clean dish towel in a single layer to dry. Before you freeze it, it must be completely dry otherwise it will rapidly develop freezer burn.

Prepare the fruit as if you were going to use it, i.e. Slice or dice fruit that will be used in a pie, roughly chop fruit that will become a smoothie and so on. In general, fruit for freezing is usually prepared as follows:

Apples / pears – core and slice or cut into chunks – peel can be removed or left on
Stone fruit (plums, nectarines, greengage, peaches, etc.) – remove the pits and slice or chunk
Cherries – remove the pits and stems, leave whole or cut in half
Berries (raspberries, blueberries, etc.) – leave whole Strawberries – hull, then slice or cut into chunks
Melons – remove the rind then cut into chunks or use a melon baller

Once the fruit has dried, line a baking sheet with parchment paper and arrange the fruit in a single layer on it. The pieces of fruit can touch a little, but avoid layering or overlapping so that the fruits can freeze separately, making them easier to remove from the freezer when you want to use them.

Put the baking tray into the freezer, careful to keep it level, and freeze for about four or five hours, until the fruit is solid. Once they are solid, package them up for long term storage. Although you can leave your fruit like this overnight, leaving them too long will encourage freezer burn to develop.

Pack your fruit into labelled freezer bags or containers. I've found it best to write the type of fruit, the weight or amount (helpful when cooking) and the date it was frozen. I freeze pumpkin and rhubarb every year and I always freeze the pumpkin in batches that are heavy enough to make two pumpkin pies. This means I am defrosting exactly what I need to use when making the pies and there is no wastage!

Make sure you get as much air as possible out of the containers (or vacuum seal). Pack the fruit into the freezer, careful to maximize your use of freezer space without damaging your packaging while keeping the containers upright.

Frozen fruit will last for around three months before it starts to develop freezer burn and grow ice crystals. Vacuum sealing will

roughly double the storage time in your freezer.

A Guide to Freezing Vegetables

Most vegetables can be frozen, though they need blanching first. We will go into blanching in more detail very shortly, as different vegetables need to be blanched for different lengths of time. The basic process is to dunk the vegetables in boiling water then after a short period of time, plunge them into ice water to cool them and stop the cooking process.

The key to successfully freezing vegetables is to make sure that as little air as possible is in your frozen produce. Contact with the air changes both the flavor and color, plus you end up with crystallized water on the fruit or vegetables.

Anything you freeze needs to be frozen in an air tight container or a heavy duty, freezer bag. Do not use lightweight sandwich bags as they will not keep the air out and your hard work will be ruined. The best way to freeze anything is to vacuum seal, which we will talk about shortly.

It is always worth turning your freezer up to maximum a few hours before you put your home-grown food in it. This will help to freeze everything as quickly as possible, which helps to reduce damage to it. Just remember to turn it back down again several hours after filling your freezer.

The majority of vegetables can be cooked straight from the freezer, put directly into boiling water. Fruit needs to thaw out at room temperature, but soft fruits and berries will turn mushy if allowed to thaw out completely. Most people will use soft berries while still partially frozen in a smoothie or with ice cream.

Blanching Vegetables
Before you freeze any vegetable, it must be blanched. This slows, or stops, the action of enzymes within the vegetable which results in the flavor or color deteriorating.

How long you blanch a vegetable for is very important – too long and it becomes mushy, too short and it won't have any effect, except for making the enzymes more active! The time also varies depending on the type of vegetable as well as its size, so if you are cutting up a vegetable, it needs to be even sized pieces.

Blanching and freezing should be done as soon as possible after harvesting in order to preserve the vegetable in peak condition. The vegetables need to be washed, drained, sorted and trimmed.
Remove any damaged or diseased parts; you can still use the rest of the vegetable if there is any damage. Cut the vegetables into the size of their desired use, e.g. Slice, dice, cut into chunks, etc.

Bring a pot of water to the boil, ensuring there is plenty of water in it. You usually end up blanching in batches as most people don't have a pot big enough to fit everything in at once! A wire basket or a coarse mesh bag helps to get the vegetables in and out of the water easily. If you don't have these, then you can use a slotted spatula but be quick about it, still being careful with the boiling water.

It is possible to steam blanch vegetables if you prefer. Boil a couple of inches of water in a steamer and then place the vegetables over the top of the boiling water in the steam in a single layer.

Put the vegetables into the boiling water and cover. The blanching time starts the moment the water returns to the boil or immediately if you are steam blanching.

After the designated time (which you will learn shortly), remove the vegetables from the boiling water and immediately immerse in cold water (below 60F). Stir them around whilst cooling to ensure they cool as fast as possible. The vegetables continue to cook once taken out of the boiling water, hence the importance of cooling them thoroughly and quickly.

Once cooled, drain the vegetables and then either freeze in a single layer on a baking tray before packaging or just put into an air tight container or freezer bag and freeze. Make sure you label the containers or bags with the weight, the name of the vegetable and the date it was frozen.

Frozen vegetables are usually fine in your freezer for between eight months to a year after freezing.

The following table shows the blanching times for some of the more common varieties of vegetable for both steam and boiling water. All times are given in minutes.

Vegetable-Boiling Water Blanching- Steam Blanching

Vegetable	Boiling Water	Steam
Asparagus – small	2	3
Asparagus – medium	3	5
Asparagus – large	4	6
Beans (green, snap or wax)	3	5
Beans (butter, lima or pinto) Small	2	3
Medium	3	5
Large	4	6
Bell Peppers (halved)	3	5
Bell Peppers (slices or rings)	2	3
Broccoli (cut into 1½" florets)	4	5
Brussels Sprouts (medium sized)	4	6
Cabbage (shredded)	1½	2½
Carrots (small & whole)	5	8
Carrots (diced or sliced)	2	3
Cauliflower (cut into 1" florets)	3	N/a
Celery	3	N/a

Corn on the cob (small)	7	10
Corn on the cob (medium)	9	13
Corn on the cob (large)	11	16
Corn kernels	4	6
Eggplant (aubergine)	4	6
Greens – collards	3	5
Greens - other	2	3
Kohlrabi (whole)	3	N/a
Kohlrabi (cubed)	1	N/a
Mushrooms (whole)	N/a	9
Mushrooms (buttons / quartered)	N/a	9
Mushrooms (sliced)	N/a	5
Okra (small	3	5
Okra (large)	4	8
Onions (the centre must be hot)	3-7	N/a
Onion rings	10-15s	N/a
Parsnips (cubed)	2	4
Peas (mange tout)	2-3	N/a
Peas (shelled)	1½ - 2½	3-5
Potatoes (new)	3-5	5-8
Rutabagas (swede)	3	5
Soybeans (green)	5	N/a

Pumpkin can be frozen but you need to cook and purée it first. Personally, I roast my pumpkin, then purée it, cool and freeze as roasted pumpkin has a much nicer taste than boiled pumpkin.

Sweet potatoes can be frozen but they have a tendency to go brown. The best way to freeze them is to either prepare it completely, e.g. Cook and mash it or cube and cook until almost done. Then soak the sweet potato in a quart of water with half a cup of lemon juice in.

Tomatoes can also be frozen by plunging the whole tomatoes into boiling water for about 30 seconds to loosen the skin and then remove them from the water. Peel and core them, then purée and freeze. Most people will freeze tomatoes by making soup or sauce with them. Tomatoes are best frozen in portion sized packages so they can easily be used in your cooking.

Vacuum Sealing Vegetables
The best way to seal food for the freezer so that it lasts and does not get freezer burn is to use vacuum sealing. You will need special plastic bags, which are thicker than normal to keep the air in, and a device to suck the air out of the bags. This does require special equipment, which is well worth the price if you are going to freeze a lot of fruit and vegetables. When properly vacuum sealed, you can easily double the storage time for fresh produce.

When vacuum sealing vegetables, they should be blanched first to kill any harmful bacteria and to destroy the enzymes that cause the food to break down. Fruit doesn't need blanching, but sometimes it can benefit from being stored in syrup. It is best to store your produce in portion sizes as you will waste less food.

For anyone who is freezing a lot of fresh fruit and vegetables, vacuum sealing is by far the best method of storage because it allows for the long-term storage of the produce whilst maintaining the quality of it. With vacuum sealing, you do not lose the taste or the

produce getting damaged by the freezer. It is well worth buying the proper equipment to vacuum seal fresh produce as it will last much better in your freezer. A good quality vacuum sealer can be bought for anywhere from $100 to $200, though ensure that whichever one you buy is easy to use and you can easily get hold of new bags.

Freezing Fresh Herbs

Most of us will end up with more fresh herbs that we can use. Although you can grow some herbs year round in your kitchen, it isn't always practical for everyone and some herbs will not grow in those conditions. Therefore, you can take the herbs that you have grown outside when they are their peak and freeze them for use for the rest of the year.

Most herbs are okay to be frozen, though some herbs are better dehydrated. Herbs such as mint, basil, chives, tarragon and lemon balm all freeze very well, though do remember that when frozen whole they will be limp when defrosted. They work well in cooking but are not so good for garnishing dishes.

Firstly, you need to pick the herbs and clean them, rinsing them under water. Avoid crushing them and dry them either in a salad spinner or by patting them dry with kitchen towel.

The easiest way to freeze herbs is to freeze the leaves individually. The leaves are stripped off the stems, cleaned and then frozen in a single layer on a cookie sheet. Once they are frozen, seal them up in a labelled freezer bag and leave in your freezer!

My favorite way to freeze herbs though is to freeze them in ice cubes. This lets me take out precise amounts to use in my cooking without having to use too much. You just put the ice cube in your dish, the water melts and you have fresh herbs!

Remove the leaves from the stem, wash them and chop as if you were using them fresh. Fill an ice cube tray half full of water, then put the herbs in each tray. I find putting a tablespoon of each herb into each compartment works well because I know exactly how much herbs will be in each ice cube.

The herbs may float, but push them under the water so they are soaked and they will freeze okay. Put the ice cube tray in the freezer and then several hours later, when it is frozen, top up the ice cube tray with water so each cube is full. Once they are fully frozen you can remove the ice cubes from the tray and put them into a labelled and dated freezer bag.

These are perfect for use in cooking stews, soups and other meals. Just put in the number of ice cubes you need, knowing that each one is a tablespoon of that herb! You can even make mixed herbs, by mixing together a variety of herbs you use in specific dishes. For example, if you regularly use basil, parsley, oregano and rosemary in

a certain quantity in a favorite dish, simply freeze that amount of the herbs in a single ice cubes ... it really speeds up cooking!

A slight variation to this is to freeze your herbs in oil, following the same process as with water, except using olive oil instead. They are used in exactly the same way when cooking.

Freezing fresh herbs is a great way to make use of the abundance of fresh herbs that grow in the summer. You can keep them frozen, where they will last for the entire year until the next harvest. Some people will freeze some herbs and dry others, see later for more information on drying, so they have the best of both worlds, using the dried herbs first.

How to Can Fruits and Vegetables

Canning, known as bottling in the UK and Europe, is the process of preserving fruits and vegetables in jars with airtight seals, usually Kilner jars. In this chapter, we will use the term canning, but it is interchangeable with bottling throughout.

The process is fairly simple, though requires some work, meaning it is usually used by the more serious preservation fan. However, anyone can do this and it is a good way to preserve the produce you have grown as it will last for months and often up to a year.

There are two main methods of canning:

Pressure Canning Water Bath Canning

Although there are other methods people use, these two methods are the most common and the easiest.

Which method you use will depend on the acidity of the food you are preserving. Not everyone is aware of the pH of food, but don't worry, it is quite easy to work out and will be explained shortly.

Foods that are low in acid, such as meat, vegetables and soups will usually have a pH of 4.6 or higher and are best preserved using a pressure canner.

Foods that are more acidic, with a pH of less than 4.6 are better preserved using a water bath canner. These include fruits and fruit based products such as jams, jellies, fruit spreads and fruit butters. Pickled vegetables can also be canned using the water bath method because the vinegar makes the food more acidic.

Tomatoes are the exception to these rules and most people recommend that they are canned using the water bath method but lemon juice is added to acidify the tomatoes.

You need to be careful when canning because certain unpleasant things, including botulism, will survive in a low acid environment. Low acid foods are preserved using the pressure canning method because the heat involved in the process kills botulism spores, ensuring the end product is safe to eat and will store well.

Always use freshly harvested produce when canning. Any fruits and vegetables which are damaged or diseased should not be canned and instead used either immediately or in the next few days. I don't

recommend cutting out the damaged parts as there may be other areas where you cannot see the damage, disease or pest and you don't want to risk it damaging your supplies. Good quality produce is going to store much better than any that is damaged or over ripe.

Guide to Pressure Canning

Pressure canning is the best way to preserve low acid foods, which includes any meats and most vegetables. You will need some equipment for this method, including:

Pressure canner
Canning jars, lids and rings Canning funnel
Jar lifter
Towels / pot holders

Firstly, your canner needs filling with water – at least three quarts is necessary, more for foods that take longer to process. You need to avoid your canner drying out as it could damage both the canner and your jars. You do not need to cover the jars with water and are aiming for pressure to build up which will generate the heat required for safe canning.

The jars do not need sterilizing before canning as they are sterilized by the temperatures reached during the canning process. However, they should be thoroughly cleaned before use. They also need to be kept warm before you fill them as, occasionally, cold jars will shatter when put in hot water. This is done by washing them in the dishwasher and leaving them in there with the door closed until you are ready to use them. Alternatively, put the jars upside down in a couple of inches of hot water. Bring the water to the boil, turn the heat off and leave the jars there until you are ready to use them.

The seals also need to be kept warm which is done by keeping them in a pan of warm water until you are ready to use them.

Put the rack on the bottom of your pressure canner and heat the water until it is hot, but not boiling. Then, maintain the temperature.

Prepare the food you are canning and fill each jar, leaving an inch head space between the top of the vegetable or meat and the top of the jar. Use a jar lifter to move the jars as they will be hot both before and after filling. Run a plastic spatula (don't use anything metallic) around the inside of the jar to remove any air bubbles. Wipe the jar's rim clean using a paper towel as any drips can allow grow bacteria when in storage.

Next, put the seals and rings on the jars and tighten so they are finger tight. Don't over-tighten them as you will struggle to get them off once the jars have cooled.

The jars are then placed on the rack of your pressure canner; make sure they do not touch each other and do not sit on the bottom of the canner. It is important that steam can circulate around the jars. It's like a jigsaw puzzle and may take a little fiddling, but it is vital to ensure your produce stores correctly.

Put the cover on your canner, make sure it is securely fitted, then heat to boiling. Steam should be venting from your canner, and allow it to do this for about ten minutes. This is very important as it pushes the air out of the canner.

Close the vent and / or put on your weighted gauge, depending on the type of canner you have. Once the right pressure is reached (check your canner instructions), turn the heat down to maintain the

pressure, adjusting the heat as necessary to keep the pressure consistent.

Now you start timing, and the time will depend on the produce you are using, make sure you adjust for altitude – more on that later on.

Keep a close eye on the pressure gauge throughout the process. If the pressure drops then you will need to start your timing again. I'd recommend staying near your pressure canner during the process. Usually, I clean up or prepare the next batch so I can keep an eye on it and make sure the correct pressure level is maintained.

Once the canning time is up, turn the heat off and leave the canner to sit until the pressure returns to zero. Once the pressure is zero, which may take a while, remove the weight or open the vent and wait a couple of minutes.

Very carefully, remove the lid, tilting it to avoid getting a face full of steam.

Using your jar lifter, take the jars out of the canner and put on a thick towel or wooden board. Remember these are extremely hot and are going to damage your kitchen work surface if put them directly on it. Leave a couple of inches between the jars so they can cool properly.

Leave the jars alone, avoiding the temptation to push down on the lids. It can take up to twelve hours for the jars to cool fully. Once they are fully cooled you can press the lids to check the seal.
The seal should have been sucked down during the cooling process and will not pop up when pressed.

You may find one or two jars that have not sealed properly. These should be put in your refrigerator and used over the next couple of weeks. Label up all your jars with the name of the produce in it and the date it was canned for reference. This ensures you know exactly what is in each jar, which is important if you are canning different varieties of the same vegetable. It also helps ensure nothing goes past its best before date and your jars are used up in the correct order.

Remember that after use, your jars should be thoroughly cleaned and sterilized before being stored away.

Cooled jars should be stored in a cool, dry, dark environment with low humidity. Avoid direct sunlight. A pantry or cupboard, away from hot water pipes, will be fine and the jars can store for a year or two, depending on the contents.

Guide to Water Bath Canning

This is a great way to can fruits, pickles, jams and other high acid fruits. Tomatoes are a special case, and we will talk about these shortly in a separate section. This is the general process for water bath canning, though it will need adjusting depending on what you are canning.

You will need a water bath canner and similar equipment to the previous method, such as canning jars, rings and lids, jar lifter, canning funnel and so on.

Start by washing and sterilizing your jars, then fill your water canner to about a third full of water and heat until it is hot, but not boiling. Technically, you don't need to sterilize jars unless your processing time is less than ten minutes, which is very rare. However, most people sterilize their jars just to be on the safe side. The jars need to be kept hot until you are ready to fill them. Warm the rings and lids too.

Prepare the food according to the recipe and fill the jar to about an inch from the top, to allow for expansion and cooling. Run a plastic spatula around the inside of the jar to remove any air bubbles, then wipe the rim and outside of the jar clean.

Put the seals on the jars and then the rings, tightening so they are finger tight. No need to over tighten them because you will struggle to loosen them once they are sealed.

The jars are then put on the canner rack, making sure they do not touch the bottom or each other. Water must be able to flow around all of the jars, and when all the jars are in the canner, they should be sat in a minimum of 2" of water.

The advantage of water bath canning is that you don't need a specialist canner – you can get away with using any large pot so long as you can keep the jars from touching the bottom of the pot.

Put the cover on the canner and then get the water to a full boil. As soon as it is boiling, start timing, though adjust for altitude if you are more than a thousand feet above sea level. Check the canner regularly, adjusting the heat as required, to keep the water on a full boil. You may need to add more boiling water to maintain the water level – don't let it stop boiling when you add more water!

Once the required time is up, turn off the heat. In some canners, you can lift the rack up out of the water, in which case do that, otherwise leave the jars for a few minutes. Then, using a jar lifter, careful remove the jars and place them in an upright position to cool. Avoid putting them directly on to a kitchen work surface as they could damage it, use a thick towel or wooden board. Make sure the jars are not touching each other and then leave them to cool.

Leave the jars alone, don't poke or prod them, allow them to cool fully, which can take as long as twelve hours. Once they have cooled, check the seals and use any that haven't sealed properly first. Label and date your jars before putting them in a cool, dark environment out of direct sunlight.

How to Sterilize Canning Jars

There are lots of different ways to sterilize canning jars and we'll talk about that for a moment here.

With pressure canning you don't need to sterilize your jars because the high heats involved will sterilize everything fully. Personally, I give everything a good wash, usually running it through the dishwasher, before I use my jars, just to ensure they are clean.

With water bath canning, so long as you are boiling for more than ten minutes, which you will do with pretty much everything, there is no need to sterilize the jars.

Jars should be well cleaned between uses. Always clean them as soon as you finish using them, rather than leaving them dirty; yes people really do that. Wash with detergent and hot water and then rinse thoroughly. Any traces of detergent on the jars can cause an unpleasant flavor or change the color of your food.

Guide to Canning Tomatoes

Tomatoes are the exception to the rules of canning because acidity levels in tomatoes are low. Water bath canning, which was traditionally used, has been discovered to allow potentially harmful bacteria to survive and grow, particularly during long term storage. New guidelines state that tomatoes need acidity adding to them in order to make them safe when canned.

For each pint of tomatoes, use one tablespoon of bottled lemon juice or a quarter of a teaspoon of citric acid. For a quart of tomatoes, use twice this; two tablespoons of bottled lemon juice or half a teaspoon of citric acid.

Most people will say that you do not need to add the lemon juice when using a pressure canner, only when using a water bath canner. However, guidelines exist in some states to add lemon juice regardless of the method of canning used.

My recommendation is that you cannot take the safety of yourself and your family too lightly and for the sake of a few dashes of lemon juice, it is better to be safe than sorry. The last thing you want to do is eat your canned tomatoes and make yourself or your family seriously ill with food poisoning. The lemon juice makes very little, if any, difference to the taste of the tomatoes, and ensures they are perfectly safe to eat.

If you are making a tomato based soup, stewed tomatoes, spaghetti sauce or adding any vegetables to tomatoes before canning then you need to use a pressure canner to store them.

Some people recommend using vinegar when canning tomatoes, instead of lemon juice. Although this is possible, the vinegar will change the taste of tomatoes and some people do not find this pleasant. Lemon juice is cheap, easily available and can be stored for some time in your refrigerator and is therefore better to use.

Pressure Canning Recipes
To help you get started, here are some recipes for common produce canned using a pressure canner. Remember, this canning method is used for low acid vegetables and meats. With any of these recipes, you can add salt to each jar before canning if you prefer. This is entirely optional and some people like additional salt adding to their vegetables, whilst others prefer to can without salt.

Canning Beetroot
Beetroots are a favorite to can. They last fairly well on the shelf, but canning ensures they are fresh and delicious for up to 12 months after harvest. Ideally you want all your beetroot to be roughly the same size as this will ensure they all cook at the same rate and you don't end up with hard pieces of beetroot in your cans.

Ingredients:

7 or 8lbs of beetroot (fresh and all about 2-3" across) 1½ teaspoons of canning or pickling salt (optional)

Method:

1) Trim the beetroot, leaving the roots and an inch of the stem to prevent the color bleeding out
2) Scrub the beetroot thoroughly to remove all dirt
3) Cook the beetroot in water for 30-45 minutes until tender (a knife will easily go all the way through) – larger beetroot will take longer to cook than the smaller ones
4) Drain the liquid and discard it

5) Cool the beetroot, either in cold water or on the side; they need to be cool enough so you can handle them
6) Once they have cooled enough, top and tail the beetroot and remove the skins
7) Slice, quarter or dice the beetroot, depending on your preference, smaller (under 1") beetroots can be left whole
8) Pack your sterile jars with the beetroot, leaving about 1" headspace at the top of each jar
9) Optional – add a teaspoon of salt per quart to each jar – this isn't necessary, but some people prefer doing this
10) Fill each jar with boiling water to about 1" from the rim, ensuring the beetroots are covered
11) Gently tap the jars on the counter top to release any air bubbles
12) Put the lids on the jars and seal them

13) The jars are carefully put in your pre-heated pressure canner, on the rack
14) Allow the canner to vent steam for 10 minutes
15) Put the weight on, close any openings and allow the pressure to build to 11 pounds
16) Once it hits 11 pounds, set the timer for 35 minutes for quart jars and 30 minutes for pint jars
17) Turn the heat off, allowing the pressure to drop to zero before you attempt to open the canner
18) Remove the jars from the canner and leave on towels or a wooden chopping board, not touching each other, to cool fully
19) Once cooled, check the seal

20) Store in an upright position in a cool, dark location

Canning Green Beans
Green beans are great when canned. Fresh, young beans are perfect for canning, but you can use older beans if you are prepared to cook them for slightly longer.

Ingredients:
2lb fresh green beans for each quart jar Water
Salt (optional)

Method:
1) Heat your pressure canner and sterilize your jars
2) Wash the beans thoroughly
3) Top and tail the beans and remove any stringy parts

4) Either leave whole (all at the same length) or cut into 2" lengths

5) Put the beans into a saucepan, cover with water and boil for 5 to 10 minutes depending on how large you have cut your beans

6) Strain the beans, then pack into jars leaving 1" headspace

7) Optional – add a teaspoon of salt to each quart jar, ½ teaspoon to each pint jar

8) Cover the beans with boiling water, leaving 1" headspace

9) Tap the jars gently on the counter top to remove any air bubbles

10) Seal the jars and put into your preheated canner

11) Process in your canner at 10 pounds of pressure

12) Pint jars require 20 minutes, quart jars require 25 minutes

13) Remove the jars from the canner, cool and check the seal before storing

Canning Corn

Fresh corn is great to can as it is a wonderful way to preserve corn for later in the year. This will store for up to a year when canned and should be refrigerated when opened.

Ingredients:
Between 10 and 19 ears of corn per quart jar Water
Salt (optional)

Method:
1) Pre-heat your canner and sterilize your jars
2) Remove the husk and silk from the corn and wash them well
3) Cut the kernels from the cob and measure them

4) For each 4 cups of corn you need 2 cups of water
5) Put the corn and water into a saucepan and bring to the boil
6) Simmer for 5 minutes then remove from the heat
7) Pack each jar with corn, leaving 1" headspace
8) Fill with boiling water, again leaving the 1" headspace
9) Tap gently on the counter top to remove any air bubbles
10) Seal the jars and then process in your canner at 10 pounds of pressure for 55 minutes if you have used pint jars and 1 hour 25 minutes if you have used quart jars
11) Allow to cool in the usual manner before storing

Canning Peppers

Peppers are very easy to can, whether you are canning chilli peppers or bell peppers. Peppers will store, when canned, for around a year, but when opened should be refrigerated and used within two or three weeks. When choosing peppers to can, use fresh, crisp peppers as they will preserve better.

Ingredients:
Peppers – all one kind or a mixture Water

Method:
1) Choose your peppers, any you like, from chilli peppers to bell peppers, just be aware that really hot peppers should be handled with gloves. Your peppers can be canned whole, sliced or chopped, though if cutting them remove all the seeds. If the peppers are left whole, cut three or four slits in the side of each one so water can get in to them
2) Pre-heat your pressure canner and sterilize your jars

3) Heat a frying pan on a medium heat, then lay the peppers on the base of the pan with the skin down. Leave for a few minutes and the skin will bubble up and blister

4) Repeat this for all of the peppers and place cooked peppers in a separate saucepan, cover with a damp cloth to cool, making the peppers easier to peel

5) Once cooled, peel off the skin (note the skins can get very tough during the canning process). Alternatively, cook the

peppers in a pre-heated oven for around 8 minutes until the skin blisters

6) Fill the jars with the peppers, leaving 1" headspace

7) Pour boiling water into the jars, ensuring the peppers are covered and the headspace retained, removing any trapped air bubbles

8) Seal the jars

9) Can at a pressure of 11lb for 35 minutes

10) Remove cans from the canner, cool, check the seals and then store

Canning Carrots

Carrots are also popular to can, whether you slice them, cut them into batons or can baby carrots whole. Use fresh carrots, removing any diseased or damaged parts. Wash them well, peel them and top and tail them before canning.

Ingredients:

4-6lbs carrots Water

Method:
1) Preheat your canner and sterilize your jars
2) Prepare the carrots and cut to size
3) Pack the carrots tightly into the cans, leaving the usual 1" headspace
4) Fill with boiling water, leaving the headspace clear and tap on the countertop to remove trapped air bubbles
5) Seal the jars
6) Process pint jars for 25 minutes at 10 pounds of pressure
7) Cool, check seals and store

Canning Pumpkin

Pumpkins are really good canned because you can use them later in the year when pumpkins are out of season and not available in the stores. Always remember to use good quality fruit with no rind or string on the fruit. Do not purée the pumpkin before canning, it must be cubed (1" cubes are recommended). The smaller, sugar or pie types, are much better for canning than the larger varieties. This process can also be followed for any summer squash.

Method:
1) Pre-heat your canner and sterilize your jars
2) Wash the pumpkin, remove the seeds, pulp and all stringy bits
3) Cut the pumpkin into 1" wide slices, peel the rind off then cut into 1" cubes
4) Boil the pumpkin cubes in water for two minutes

5) Fill the jars with pumpkin, leaving 1" headspace and tap on the countertop to remove air bubbles

6) Seal the jars

7) Process in your pressure canner at 11lb pressure for 55 minutes for pint jars or 90 minutes for quart jars

Canning Asparagus

Asparagus is another popular vegetable to can. Use fresh spears that have tight tips. They need to be between 4 and 6 inches long, depending on the size of your jars. About 24 pounds of asparagus will fill seven quart jars, approximately.

Method:

1) Wash the asparagus, trim the bottom and trim off any of the tougher scales

2) Cut the spears to the size of your jars, remembering to leave a 1" headspace in each jar

3) You can pack the asparagus in the jars raw or you can boil it for around 3 minutes in water

4) Pack the jars and fill with boiling water, leaving the 1" headspace

5) Tap the jars on the counter top to remove air bubbles

6) Seal the jars

7) Process in your canner at 11lb of pressure for 30 minutes for pint jars and 40 minutes for quart jars

8) Remove from canner, cool, check seals and store

Canning Potatoes

Potatoes are also very good canned. They are easy to store and will store for up to a year in a cool, dark place. Can new potatoes halved or whole and other potatoes cut into cubes. I'd recommend bathing the potatoes for a few minutes in an ascorbic acid solution after peeling and chopping to prevent darkening through oxidization.

Method:
1) Wash and peel the potatoes
2) Cut to size

3) Boil the potatoes – 10 minutes for whole, new potatoes and around 2-3 minutes for ½" cubes
4) Drain
5) Fill the jars with fresh water (do not reuse water from earlier), leaving the 1" headspace
6) Tap on the counter top to remove air bubbles
7) Seal the jars
8) Process at 11lb for 35 minutes in pint jars or 40 minutes in quart jars
9) Remove from the canner, cool, check seals and store

Water Bath Canning Recipes

Here are some recipes and methods for canning the high acid fruits that are processed using the water bath method. Do not can vegetables and low acid vegetables using these method as you run the risk of dangerous bacteria growing during storage. Tomatoes will be discussed separately shortly.

Grape Juice

Fresh grape juice can be canned and used fresh or in cooking. If you grow grapes, this is a great way to preserve the juice for use later in the year. Typically, about 24 pounds of grapes will produce enough juice for 7 quarts, with around 16 pounds being sufficient for 9 pints. Remember, you want sweet, firm grapes with a good color.

Method:
1) Wash the grapes and remove the stems
2) Put the grapes in a large saucepan and cover with boiling water
3) Simmer on a low heat until the skins are soft
4) Strain through a jelly bag (this may take some time)
5) Refrigerate the juice for 1 to 2 days
6) Carefully remove the juice from the fridge and pour off the clear liquid and keep, discarding the sediment that will have formed (you can strain through coffee filter paper to make the juice clearer)
7) Pour the juice into a saucepan and sweeten to taste
8) Heat and stir until all the sugar has dissolved
9) Bring to the boil, stirring often
10) Fill the jars, leaving just ¼" headspace
11) Seal the jars
12) Process in your canner for 10 minutes for pint or quart jars

Rhubarb

Canning is a great alternative to freezing for rhubarb, particularly if you want chopped rhubarb rather than puréed. When canning, do not purée your rhubarb, it should be chopped instead. Around a pound of rhubarb will be enough to fill a pint jar.

Method:

1) Preheat your canner and sterilize your jars
2) Wash and trim the rhubarb
3) Cut into ½" to 1" pieces (removing any stringy bits)
4) Measure how much rhubarb you have (in quarts)
5) Put the rhubarb in a saucepan together with ½ cup of sugar for each quart of rhubarb
6) Do not heat yet, leave the rhubarb to stand until you see juice in the pan
7) Gently bring the pan to a boil
8) Fill the jars with rhubarb and liquid leaving ½" headspace
9) Use a plastic spatula to remove trapped air bubbles, adding more rhubarb if necessary
10) Wipe the jar clean and seal
11) Process for 20 minutes, keeping the water level about 2" above the jars
12) Remove, cool, check seals and store

Apple Sauce

Apple sauce is an excellent way to preserve a glut of apples for later in the year. You can make the sauce as sweet or tart as you want using a combination of sweet and tart apples. Around three pounds of apples will be enough for a quart of apple sauce. Apple slices can be canned in a similar manner, though both quart and pint jars are processed for 25 minutes.

Method:
1) Wash, peel and core the apples and cut into slices
2) Put the apple slices in an ascorbic acid solution to prevent them going brown
3) Add ½ cup of water plus the apple slices into a large saucepan
4) Heat and cook until tender, stirring often. This can take anything from 5 to 20 minutes depending on the type of apple and how ripe they are
5) Either run through a food mill or sieve, if you prefer a smooth sauce or mash roughly with a wooden spoon if you prefer a chunkier sauce
6) Taste the sauce and add sugar if necessary (about 1/8 cup per quart of sauce is recommended)
7) Bring the sauce back to the boil, stirring often, ensuring any sugar is dissolved
8) Fill the jars with sauce, leaving ½" headspace
9) Wipe the jars and seal
10) Process for 20 minutes for pint jars and 25 minutes for quart jars

11) Cool, test seal and store

Pears

Pears are good to can because they ripen all at once and often do not store well. You should choose pears that are ready to eat rather than too ripe. Approximately 17 pounds of pears will fill 7 quart jars. Around 11 pounds will be sufficient for 9 pint jars.

Method:
1) Preheat your canner and sterilize your jars
2) Wash and peel the pears
3) Cut in half lengthways and remove the core – store in an ascorbic acid solution to prevent browning
4) Boil the pears in water for 5 minutes (note you can boil and pack in apple juice, a syrup or white grape juice if you prefer)
5) Fill the jars with the pears and the liquid they were cooked in, leaving ½" headspace, and seal the jars
6) Process for 25 minutes for pint jars and 30 minutes for quart jars
7) Remove from canner, cool, test seal and store

Plums

Again, if you grow plums you can end up with a glut of them at harvest time, so this is a good way to store them for use later in the year. It is best to choose good quality, ripe, firm plums to can, avoiding any diseased or damaged fruits. For 7 quart jars you will need about 14 pounds of plums and for 9 pint jars you will need

about 9 pounds of plums. Plums can be packed in a syrup or in water.

Method:
1) Preheat your canner and sterilize your jars
2) Remove stems from the plums and wash well
3) Can whole (prick the skin twice with a fork to stop the plums from splitting) or half them and remove the stones
4) Boil the plums in water for 2 minutes
5) Turn the heat off, cover the saucepan and leave to stand for 30 minutes
6) Fill the jars with the cooking liquid and plums, leaving ½" headspace and seal the jars
7) Process for 25 minutes for pint jars and 30 minutes for quart jars
8) Remove from the canner, cool, check seal and store

Cherries

Cherries work well when canned and look fantastic on the shelf. As always, you need good quality, firm fruit that isn't damaged. To fill 7 quart jars you will need in the region of 17 pounds of cherries and to fill 9 pint jars you will need approximately 11 pounds of fruit.

Cherries can be boiled and packed in syrup or water.

Method:
1) Preheat your canner and sterilize your jars
2) Remove stems and wash the cherries
3) Remove stones, if required, but if you do then store in an ascorbic acid solution until ready to proceed to prevent discoloration

4)   If canning whole, prick twice on opposite sides with a needle to prevent splitting

5)   Boil the cherries in ½ cup of water (or syrup) for each quart of fruit, then remove from the heat

6)   Alternatively, you can raw pack your cherries but they need processing in your canner for 30 minutes (both pint and quart jars)

7)   Fill the jars, leaving ½" headspace, with cherries and liquid from the pan

8)   Seal the jars

9)   Process cooked cherries for 20 minutes, if using pint jars, and 25 minutes if using quart jars

Altitude Adjustments for Canning

You may, or may not be aware, that the higher up you live, the lower the atmospheric pressure is, which changes the boiling point of water! When canning, if you live over 1000 feet above sea level, you need to change the timings when canning food. This will only affect a small number of people, but you need to be aware of it to ensure you are safely storing your food.

As the boiling point of water is lower than 212F / 100C above 1000 feet, you need to increase the processing time to compensate for the lower temperatures.

A pressure canner is additionally affected by atmospheric pressure as it needs to hit 240F / 115C in order to prevent botulism.

Therefore, at higher altitudes you need to increase the amount of pressure rather than change the time.

Firstly, you need to know high above sea level you are. This is easily done by either searching online for your location and the word 'altitude' or going to a site like www.veloroutes.org, clicking on elevation and entering your location.

For most of us, this isn't going to have any effect, but for anyone living in a more mountainous area, they will need to change how they can produce.

For pressure canners, the altitude adjustments are as follows:

Altitude (in Feet)	Dial Gauge Canner	Weighted Gauge Canner
0 – 1000	10	10
1001 – 2000	11	15
2001 – 4000	12	15
4001 – 6000	13	15
6001 – 8000	14	15
8001 – 10000	15	15

For water bath canning, the following adjustments are made:

Altitude (in Feet)	Increase to Processing Time
0 – 3000	5 mins
3001 – 6000	10 mins
6001 – 8000	15 mins
8001 – 10000	20 mins

Although this may seem trivial, it is vitally important if you want to ensure that your canning is safe and the produce will last. For most people this isn't going to be an issue, but for anyone who lives at a higher altitude, it is something they need to be aware of.

Drying Fruits and Vegetables

A very good way of storing fruits and vegetables, perhaps more so with fruits rather than vegetables, is to dry them. Dried fruit is excellent for cooking with or adding to yogurt, granola, cereal or just eating raw as a snack. You can dry it in your oven (it needs a low setting of 170F which not all ovens have) or you can buy a specially made dehydrator which is a clever electronic device that does it all for you.

You can dry your home-grown produce or you can buy fruit in bulk when it is in season and cheap, drying it for use later in the year.

Fruit should be dried as soon as you can after it has been harvested. The longer you leave it, the more it will continue to ripen and perhaps go past its best. You need fruit that is ripe, but not overripe and definitely none that are bruised. Anything that is overripe or bruised should be used immediately or in the next few days rather than dried.

Be aware that if you are drying a batch of produce, you cannot add fresh produce to a batch that is part way through the drying process. You need to start a new batch with the new produce.

If you are using fruit such as apples and pears then they must be peeled before use. Berries can be dried whole, though remove the stones from any fruit that has them.

Wash your fruit well before starting the drying process and then cut them into the desired sizes. Try to keep the sizes uniform because the fruit will dry evenly and you won't end up with squishy spots.
Fruit that doesn't dry fully can end up growing mold and rotting, which can spoil an entire batch.

Using some non-stick baking sheets, arrange your fruit in a single layer so they are not touching each other. Put them in to your oven, preheated to 170F (about 75C). Leave the over door slightly open and stir the fruit every half hour so that the air can circulate fully.

How long the fruit will take to dry will depend on the type of fruit and the size of it. When it is dried properly, it will be chewy but not crispy (over-done) or squishy (under done). This can take anything from four to as much as eight hours to completely dry.

Once dried, remove the trays from the oven and allow to stand for 12 hours before storing in air-tight containers. Store in a cool, dark, dry place where they will last anything for 6 to 12 months. Vacuum sealing will extend the storage time, usually doubling it.

Using a Dehydrator

A dehydrator is a way to dry your fruit using an electronic device. It is a lot easier than an oven in that you do not need to keep checking it and can switch it on and leave it to it. However, not everyone owns a dehydrator and not everyone has room on their kitchen counter for another gadget. Saying that, they are very useful devices and when you start to dry your own fruit you will be very glad you bought one!

As well as fruit, some people will dehydrate vegetables that are used in stews such as potatoes, corn, peas, carrots and so on. These are blanched before dehydrating for the reasons explained earlier in this book, following the same guidelines.

Fruit is prepared as normal for drying, though any fruits that oxidise in air, e.g. Apples and pears, can be treated with some lemon juice to help retain their color and not turn brown.

With an electronic dehydrator it is easier for you to add salt, sugar or even spices to the fruit to give it some flavor. Try scattering some cinnamon over your apple rings, or even some nutmeg and ground cloves for a delicious dried snack.

Your dehydrator will have a number of trays, put your sliced fruit on the trays, making sure they are in a single layer. The fruit must not touch each other so that they air can circulate around the fruit and dry it properly. Often where the fruit touches you end up with squishy bits where it hasn't dried out properly.

Your owner's manual will tell you how long to run your dehydrator. It depends on the type of fruit you are drying and the size of it. The process will take anywhere from 8 to 12 hours, but does not need you in attendance the whole time.

Once the time is up, remove a slice of fruit to check whether it is fully dry, allow it to cool and then feel it. It should feel dry to the touch.
Cut a couple of pieces of fruit (choose the larger ones) and check the edges for moisture beads. If either of these tests indicate that the fruit isn't dry enough then put it back in the dehydrator for more time.

When you are happy that the fruit is completely dry, leave it for up to an hour, until it is cool to the touch and then put in air tight jars for storage. Store in a cool, dark, dry location where it will last for six months to a year.

For fruit, initially pack them loosely in jars, shaking every day for about a week, making sure any moisture is evenly distributed between the slices. If you notice any condensation on the inside of the jar, the fruit needs to go back into the dehydrator for further drying.

Dried Fruit Recipes
There are lots of recipes using dried fruit as it can be used in all sorts of different dishes. Here are some of my favorite recipes using dried fruit.

Fruit & Nut Granola
This is a simple recipe that you can adjust to use whatever dried fruit you have to hand. I've used raisins and mixed fruit in the recipe, but substitute whatever you have, feeling free to increase the quantities to make a fruitier granola.

Ingredients:
4 cups rolled oats
1 cup dry milk powder (zero fat is best) 1 cup dried mixed fruit (chopped)
¾ cup brown sugar (packed)
½ cup raisins
½ cup walnuts (chopped)
½ cup canola oil
¼ cup water

¼ cup wheat germ (toasted)

3 teaspoons ground cinnamon 1 teaspoon vanilla extract

Method:

1) Preheat your oven to 275F / 135C

2) Mix together the milk powder, fruit, oats, cinnamon, wheat germ and walnuts in a large bowl

3) Put the water and brown sugar into a small saucepan, heating over a medium heat to a boil

4) Remove the saucepan from the heat and mix in the vanilla and oil

5) Pour this over the oat mixture and stir until thoroughly mixed in

6) Pour this into a 15 x 10 x 1" baking pan, and make sure it is spread evenly

7) Bake for between 35 and 45 minutes then remove from the oven

8) Stir in the raisins and allow to cool, stirring occasionally

9) Once cooled, store in an airtight container

Dried Fruit Stuffing

This is a lovely stuffing mix that you can use with meat, particularly chicken and turkey. It makes for a much more interesting stuffing than the usual sage and onion that is served up.

Ingredients:

6oz pack of stuffing mix

½ cup cranberries (dried)

½ cup pitted plums (dried and chopped)

½ cup apricots (dried and chopped) 1/3 cup slivered almonds (toasted)

Method:

1)   Make the stuffing mix according to the instructions on the package

2)   Add the dried fruits when you add the contents of the package

3)   The almonds are stirred in prior to serving

Fruity Granola

This is another granola recipe that really works well with the chewy dried fruit. Feel free to adjust the fruit, spices and nuts to use your favorite varieties.

Ingredients:

9oz / 250g rolled oats (use rye or spelt if you prefer) 3½oz / 100g hazelnuts (chopped)

2½oz / 75g flaked coconut

8 – 10 dried figs (coarsely chopped) 8 Medjool dates (coarsely chopped)

4 tablespoons coconut oil

4 tablespoons maple syrup

1 tablespoon ground cinnamon 1 teaspoon ground vanilla

½ teaspoon ground cardamom

Large handful of mulberries (can substitute with other berries) Handful dried cranberries

Pinch of salt

Method:
1) Preheat your oven to 350F / 175C / Gas mark 4

2) In a saucepan, simmer the coconut oil and maple syrup together
3) Remove from heat then mix in the oats, coconut, salt and hazelnuts until well combined
4) Spread on a baking sheet and cook for 20 to 25 minutes, stirring every five minutes to ensure everything is evenly cooked
5) Remove from oven when crispy and golden
6) Pour the mixture into a bowl, mixing in the dried fruit and spices
7) Leave to cool completely before storing in an air-tight container

Raisin Radicchio Salad

The bitterness of the radicchio is wonderfully offset by the sweet raisins to make a delicious salad that is good any time of the year.

Salad Ingredients:
Head of purple radicchio 3 heads of endive
½ cup / 120ml white balsamic vinegar (or white wine vinegar) 1 tablespoon sugar
2oz / 50g raisins (golden work well, but any you've made will do)

Dressing Ingredients:
3 tablespoons walnut oil
1 tablespoon white balsamic vinegar Salt and pepper to taste

Method:

1) Tear the radicchio leaves into large pieces
2) Separate the endive leaves from the heart, then cut the heart lengthwise in half
3) Warm the vinegar over a low heat until it simmers, then add the raisins and simmer, on a low heat, for about five minutes
4) Remove from heat and leave to cool, removing the raisins from the vinegar and putting to one side
5) Just before serving, mix together all of the dressing ingredients in a large bowl
6) Add the leaves and raisins to the bowl and toss, ensuring everything is thoroughly coated
7) Serve on a large plate
8) Optionally, garnish with some micro greens or toasted nuts (walnuts or pecans)

Sticky Fig Puddings

This is a lovely dessert that is great freshly cooked but can be frozen or kept for five days in your refrigerator.

Pudding Ingredients:

9oz / 250g soft dried figs (roughly chopped) 9oz / 250g self-raising flour

9oz / 250g soft brown sugar

3½oz / 100g unsalted butter (softened and diced) plus extra for greasing

½ pint / 300ml water 3 eggs

1 teaspoon bicarbonate of soda Pinch of ground cinnamon Cream or ice cream to serve

Butterscotch Sauce Ingredients: 10½oz / 300g soft brown sugar 3½oz / 100g unsalted butter
1 cup / 250ml cream (can use water if you prefer)
¼ cup / 60ml brandy (optional)

Method:
1) Preheat your oven to 400F / 200C / gas mark 6
2) Grease eight 1 cup / 250ml moulds or oven proof cups
3) Boil the figs together with the water and bicarbonate of soda, simmering on a low heat until softened, around five minutes
4) Remove the pan from the heat, stir in the butter so it melts
5) Add the sugar, stirring continually until it has dissolved
6) Beat the eggs and then add to the saucepan together with the flour and cinnamon, stirring until well combined
7) Divide the mixture evenly between the cups
8) Put the cups into a large roasting tray, filling the tray with water so it is halfway up the side of the cups
9) Cover the whole tray with foil, sealing the edges to keep the steam in
10) Bake for 45 minutes
11) To make the sauce, melt the sugar and butter together over a medium heat, stirring until the mixture starts to bubble
12) Remove from the heat and stir in the brandy

13) Return to the heat, stirring in the cream until the sauce is smooth

14) Keep the sauce warm until serving

15) Empty the puddings out of the mold, pour over sauce and serve with cream or ice cream

Warm Kale Salad

This is a lovely salad to make during the cooler months when you are picking kale from the garden.

Ingredients:

1   large apple (peeled, cored and chopped)

8oz / 225g kale (ribs and stems removed, roughly chopped) 1½oz / 40g dried cranberries

2   tablespoons unsalted butter

¼ teaspoon salt

¼ teaspoon ground cinnamon

Method:

1) Put the butter into a large frying pan and melt

2) Then add the cranberries, apples, salt and cinnamon

3) Fry, stirring often, for about eight minutes, until the apples are soft

4) Add the kale and cook for another couple of minutes until it is tender

5) Serve warm or chilled, as preferred

Dried Cherry Hot Toddy

A traditional drink when you are feeling under the weather, this is usually made with whisky or bourbon, diluted with hot water then sweetened. Enjoy this variation on the classic drink.

Ingredients:
¾ cup / 180ml boiling water
¼ cup / 60ml rye whisky (or any dark liquor) 2" / 5cm lime zest peeling
4 dried cherries
1	teaspoon sugar

Method:
1)	Stir together the sugar, cherries and zest in a glass
2)	Add the liquor
3)	Pour over the boiling water
4)	Stir until the sugar is dissolved and serve

Welsh Cakes

These are lovely cakes that can be made with a variety of different fruits, depending on what you have to hand. Adding dried apricots, dates, walnuts, white or dark chocolate can really make this even more interesting! Try the basic recipe and then add other ingredients to make them perfect for you!

Ingredients:
9oz / 250g self-raising flour
4½oz / 125g butter (good quality is preferred)

3½oz / 100g sultanas (try half and half dried apricots and white chocolate or milk chocolate and dried cranberries)

2½oz / 75g caster sugar 1 egg

Pinch of mixed spice

Method:

1) In a bowl, rub together the flour and butter until it turns into a crumb like mixture
2) Mix in the caster sugar
3) Add the egg, then stir until thoroughly combined
4) Use your hands to roll the dough into a ball in the bowl
5) Roll out the dough to ½" thick on a floured surface
6) Using a cookie cutter, cut the dough out in circle shapes, re-rolling the dough until you've used it all up
7) Heat a frying pan, using no oil or butter
8) Put each dough circle in the frying pan and cook over a medium heat until brown on either side
9) Sprinkle with caster sugar, serving whilst still warm

Pickling Fruits & Vegetables

A popular way to preserve your fruits and vegetables is by pickling. This works very well for a wide variety of produce from onions to cucumbers to cauliflower and more.

The basic process is very simple, the fruits or vegetables are put into jars, covered with vinegar and then sealed and stored. The nice thing about pickling is that the shelf life is quite long. The vinegar stops bacteria from forming and so some items can store for months and up to a year, and still be edible.

The exact process is slightly more complex, but once you start pickling, you will get addicted! If you aren't sure if you like pickled vegetables, get some from a supermarket and try them. Yours will taste much better, but they will give you an idea of what they are like. Most people are familiar with pickled onions, gherkins (pickled baby cucumbers) and perhaps even pickled red cabbage or beetroot (perhaps more popular in the UK than the USA). However, as you are about to find out, there is a lot more pickling potential!

How to Pickle Fruits & Vegetables

Pickling is surprisingly quick and requires a lot less work than many of the other methods of storage. You can buy pre-made pickling vinegar or you can make your own. Most people do a combination of the two as making your own requires boiling vinegar and spices which can be, shall we say, somewhat aromatic.

It's best to pickle fresh, undamaged vegetables. Any that are bruised are better used in a soup or served fresh. You can pickle pretty much any vegetable, cherry tomatoes are pickled whole, carrots can be sliced or turned into matchsticks, green vegetables can be sliced and so on. There's a lot of different ways of preparing your vegetables for picking and it is up to you based on how you like them! Over time you will also develop a pickling spice of your own that you prefer, though the basic spiced pickle recipes included here are a great starting point.

When preparing vegetables for pickling, the following guidelines will be helpful:

Blanch – green beans, asparagus, cauliflower, other brassicas Peel – carrots
Cut into Matchsticks – cucumbers, carrots Leave Whole – onions, gherkins
Slice Thinly – ginger, beetroot, red cabbage, onion, summer squashes, cucumbers

A very basic brine (pickling vinegar) recipe is simple equal parts of water and vinegar. You can use normal, brown (malt) vinegar, apple cider, white wine vinegar, rice vinegar, white vinegar or whatever you prefer. The fancy vinegars are good for giving flavor, but the pickled vegetables don't tend to store as long. You can buy specific pickling vinegars, which have a higher level of acidity and are better for long term storage.

To make the pickles really flavorsome, you need to add some spices to the brine. You may have eaten dill pickles, which are baby cucumbers in a pickle that has had dill seed, red pepper flakes and garlic added to it! There are lots of potential recipes and we'll talk about some in a little while, but the beauty of this is you can make them to your taste.

Some of the popular herbs and spices used in pickling include:

Fresh Herbs – rosemary, oregano, dill and thyme are very popular
Dried Herbs – as above but marjoram also works well
Garlic Cloves – slice for a strong flavor or smash for a milder flavor
Garlic Powder – has a much stronger taste than fresh garlic so be careful
Fresh Ginger – peel or slice thinly
Whole Spices – including coriander seeds, peppercorns (any color), mustard seeds, red pepper flakes, chilli flakes

Ground Spices – both smoked paprika and turmeric add taste and color

When pickling, you will need jars that have an air-tight seal on them. Usually pint jars are used, but you can use bigger ones – just be aware that you don't want a jar too big because once opened, the pickles can go off and large jars can take some time to consume.
You also need jars that will fit in your refrigerator as they need keeping cool once opened.

The jars, lids and any sealing rings need to be washed thoroughly before use in warm soapy water and then rinsed thoroughly.

Remember to clean them again after use too so they aren't stored dirty.

Prepare the vegetables before pickling, meaning wash and dry them, cut them to size and so on. Then you put the herbs and spices you are using into your jars and pack in the vegetables, leaving about ½" headspace from the rim of the jar. Although you want to pack them in tightly, don't bruise or squash them. It can be a little bit of a jigsaw puzzle to get the vegetables in, but squeeze in as many as you can.

The pickling liquid needs to be made now. You usually add equal parts of vinegar and water, though some people prefer to just use vinegar. Stir in salt and sugar, if you are using them, and bring the mixture to a boil, stirring often. You need to carefully pour this over the vegetables until they are covered, leaving the ½" gap at the top.

Finally, before sealing, you need to remove any trapped air bubbles from the jar. If you do not remove these, you are creating an environment that could allow bacteria to grow. Very carefully, the vinegar is hot, tap the jars on your counter top which will dislodge the air bubbles and bring them to the top. You may need to add more of the pickling vinegar to top up the jar.

Generic Pickling Recipe

This pickling recipe is good for any type of vegetable and is a good, general purpose method. More specific ones will follow, but this gives you a good starting point and you can adjust this recipe as you see fit.

Ingredients:

1lb fresh vegetables (tomatoes, cucumbers, carrots, green beans, etc.)

2	springs of fresh herbs (e.g. Dill, rosemary or thyme)

1 – 2 teaspoons whole spices (e.g. Coriander seeds, mustard seeds, whole peppercorns)

1	teaspoon dried herbs or ground spices

2	garlic cloves (sliced or smashed depending on preference) 1 cup vinegar

1 cup water

1 tablespoon sale

1	tablespoon granulated sugar 2 x 1 pint pickling jars

Method:

1)	Wash, rinse and dry the jars
2)	Prepare the vegetables, cutting to size
3)	Equally divide the herbs, garlic and spices between the two jars
4)	Equally divide the vegetables between the two jars, to ½" below the rim, packing tightly
5)	Put the water, vinegar, sugar and salt into a small saucepan on a high heat and boil, stirring to dissolve the sugar and salt
6)	Once fully dissolved, pour the mixture over the vegetables
7)	Remove any trapped air bubbles and top up if necessary
8)	Seal the jars, ensuring the lids are on tight but not over-tight
9)	Allow to cool, then refrigerate, leaving for a minimum of 48 hours before opening

Using this recipe, the pickled vegetables can be stored in your refrigerator for up to two months. If you follow the process for canning then you can store them at room temperature unopened.

A lot of pickled vegetables benefit from being stored for two or three months before opening. This gives the flavor a chance to really develop and permeate the vegetables. At the very least, leave them for a couple of weeks, but if you can resist temptation longer, then the flavor will improve.

Pickling is one of the safest ways to preserve food because the high acidity levels in the vinegar prevents mold or bacteria growing. Plus, you are not going to have jars exploding during the canning process. It is really easy and pickled vegetables are great to serve with salads or eat by themselves.

Pickling Recipes

Here are some of my favorite pickling recipes. They are all easy to make and you can adjust the vinegar and spices according to your personal preferences. I've included a couple of pickling vinegar ideas as well.

Pickled Onions

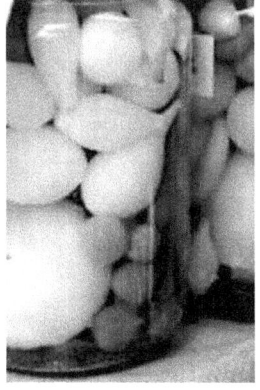

These are very popular with salads, particularly the English ploughman's salad. They can be made from any type of onion, pickling onion, baby onion or shallot, as used here. This recipe will make two good sized jars and the resulting onions are fantastic with cold meats and cheese.

Ingredients:

18oz / 500g small shallots 7oz / 200g clear honey 2oz / 50g salt

2   cups / 500ml malt (brown) vinegar

Method:

1)   Put the onions in a glass, heatproof bowl cover with boiling water
2)   Once cooled, trim the tops and roots, then peel
3)   Stir in the salt, cover and leave overnight
4)   Rinse the onions and dry
5)   Mix the vinegar and honey in a saucepan and heat gently to dissolve the honey, avoid boiling
6)   Carefully pack the onions into clean, sterile jars
7)   Fill the jars with the hot vinegar, tapping on the counter top to remove air bubbles
8)   Seal and leave to cool

9) Leave for one month, though better if you can wait two, and refrigerate once opened

Pickled Beetroot

Another English favorite, this is great with a salad and an ideal use for a glut of beetroot. This too works well with cheese and cold meats.

Ingredients:

2.2lb / 1kg Beetroot (coloured beetroot works very well) 3½oz / 100g light brown soft sugar
3 cups / 700ml white wine vinegar plus an additional 3½ tablespoons
Vegetable oil 10 cloves
2 bay leaves
1 tablespoon mustard seeds (yellow)

1 tablespoon coriander seeds
1 tablespoon black peppercorns 4-5 teaspoons sea salt
Pinch of dried chilli flakes Several mace blade pieces

Method:
1) Wash the beetroot and trim the roots and leaves to 1" long
2) Rub each one with a tablespoon of vegetable oil, wrap individually in tin foil then roast for an hour (until tender) in your oven at 400F / 200C / gas mark 6
3) Remove from oven and cool before peeling and cutting into wedges
4) Put all the whole spices into a medium sized saucepan

5) Cook over a low heat, stirring often, until they become aromatic
6) Add the chilli flakes and bay leaf, stir then pour in the sugar and vinegar
7) Stir and simmer until the sugar is dissolved
8) Pack the beetroot wedges into jars, adding a teaspoon of sea salt to each one
9) Pour the hot vinegar into the jars, covering the beetroot
10) Seal and store for two weeks before opening

Pickled Red Cabbage

Another great use for a glut that is lovely with cheese, meats and salads.

Ingredients:

18oz / 500g shredded red cabbage 14oz / 400g white sugar
5oz / 140g sea salt
2   cups / 500ml cider vinegar
¾ cup / 200ml red wine 6 bay leaves
2 tablespoons mustard seed (yellow) 2 teaspoons whole black peppercorns

Method:
1) Put the shredded cabbage into a colander, sprinkle with salt and leave for three hours
2) Drain, wash thoroughly and pat dry using paper towels
3) Using a large saucepan, simmer the vinegar, sugar, wine, bay leaves and peppercorns until reduced by about half
4) Put to one side for ten minutes to allow the flavors to mix

5) Strain the vinegar through a sieve into a bowl, discarding the bay leaves and peppercorns
6) Put both the mustard seeds and cabbage into a large bowl, pouring the vinegar over it
7) Stir well, put into sterile jars and seal
8) Will store for about a month in your refrigerator

Pickled Eggs

Another popular dish with salads and one that is definitely worth trying.

Ingredients

12 hard-boiled eggs (peeled) 2 medium onions (chopped)
4 cups / 1 litre malt (brown) vinegar 1/3 cup / 65g white (granulated) sugar 1 tablespoon pickling spices
1 teaspoon salt

Method:
1) Put the eggs into a large, sterile jar
2) Put the rest of the ingredients into a large saucepan and boil for five minutes
3) Pour the mixture over the eggs
4) Seal, leave to cool then refrigerate and use

Dill Pickled Cucumbers

Another great pickle, very popular in burgers and salads. You will be familiar with these as they are similar to shop bought gherkins or pickles, but much nicer!

Ingredients:
2.2lbs / 1kg small or ridged cucumbers 3½oz /100g white (granulated) sugar 3oz / 85g sea salt
3 cups / 700ml white wine vinegar plus 3½ tablespoons 10 cloves
2 bay leaves
1 tablespoon mustard seeds (yellow) 1 tablespoon coriander seeds

1 tablespoon black peppercorns 4-5 teaspoons sea salt
Pinch of dried chilli flakes Several mace blade pieces Handful of dill sprigs

Method:
1) Slice the cucumbers (or cut them into matchsticks)
2) Layer in a large bowl with the sea salt, cover and leave overnight
3) The next day drain away any liquid and rinse well
4) Put the whole spices into a saucepan and cook for a few minutes, stirring often, until they become aromatic
5) Add the bay leaves and chilli flakes before adding the sugar and vinegar
6) Continue to heat, stirring often, until the sugar has dissolved, then simmer for a minute
7) Add the dill sprigs
8) Put the cucumbers into sterile jars, cover the vinegar and seal

9) These are ready to eat in two weeks but do benefit from longer in the jars

Pickled Walnuts

An interesting dish that is unusual and definitely worth a try. You can buy walnuts or you may find them growing wild. You need to be careful handling the walnuts as they contain a juice that is a strong natural dye. It will dye anything it comes into contact with a dark, espresso brown color and is very difficult to remove. Wear gloves

when handling the walnuts and work on a surface that they cannot damage. This is best made before the hard shell forms within the walnuts.

Ingredients:
2lbs / 1.8kg fresh walnuts 16½oz / 470g dark brown sugar 7½oz / 215g salt
4 cups / 950ml malt vinegar
1 tablespoon fresh root ginger (grated) 1 teaspoon ground cloves
1   teaspoon ground allspice
½ teaspoon ground cinnamon

Method:
1) Wearing gloves, pierce each walnut a few times with a fork
2) Put into a bucket and cover with water
3) Stir in the salt and soak for a week
4) Drain, cover with water, add the salt and soak for another week

5) Drain the walnuts and then put on trays in an airy place to dry for 3 to 5 days, when they have all turned black they are ready to pickle
6) Put the vinegar, sugar, cloves, cinnamon, ginger and allspice into a large saucepan and bring to the boil
7) Add the walnuts and simmer for 15 minutes
8) Remove from the heat and cool
9) Put the walnuts into sterile jars and cover with the liquid
10) Seal and store in the refrigerator

Quick Pickling Vinegar

This is a very quick and easy pickling vinegar you can make which can be used to pickled any vegetable.

Ingredients:
2 pints / 1.1litres malt (brown) vinegar 2" / 50mm cinnamon stick
3 bay leaves
2 teaspoons allspice
1 teaspoon mustard seed 1 teaspoons whole cloves
1 teaspoon whole black peppercorns

Method:
1) Tie the spices into a muslin bag
2) Put the vinegar and spices into a heatproof bowl
3) Put the bowl over a saucepan of water (double boiled method) and cover the bowl with a plate to retain flavor
4) Boil the water then remove the saucepan from the heat

5) Leave for around three hours to steep
6) Strain the vinegar, cool and use

Home-Made Pickling Vinegar

This is another great pickling vinegar recipe which is good for pickling anything. I rather like the variety of spices in this as it gives the vegetables a more rounded taste.

Ingredients:

4 cups / 1¾ litre malt (brown), red or white wine vinegar

½oz / 15g mustard seeds 1 dried chilli (seeded)

1 bay leaf

1 mace blade

1 slice fresh ginger

1 tablespoon allspice berries

1 tablespoon black peppercorns Cloves & garlic to taste

Method:
1) Bruise the spices before tying them into a muslin bag
2) Boil in the vinegar for 10 minutes
3) Remove from heat, leaving the bag in until cooled
4) Once cooled use the vinegar for pickling

British Pickling Vinegar Recipe

This is a very British spice mixture, used to make pickled onions and gherkins, but good for any vegetables. If you want a more intense flavor, crush the spices before putting them into the muslin bag.

Ingredients:

4 dried red chillies 3 dried bay leaves 1" cinnamon stick 1" dried ginger root

1 tablespoon black peppercorns

1 tablespoon coriander seeds 1 tablespoon cloves

1 tablespoon coriander seeds

Method:

1) Tie the spices in a muslin bag and use when pickling any vegetable

2) Boil in 4 cups / 1¾ litre of vinegar for ten minutes, remove from heat and leave to cool with the bag in

3) Alternatively, a cold spice vinegar can be made by putting the spices in a jar of vinegar and leaving for two days

Making Jams and Jellies

Jams and jellies are a fantastic way of preserving fruit and a lovely reminder of summer through the bleak winter months. Jams and jellies are actually different, in a jelly the fruit comes from juice but in a jam the fruit is

whole or crushed fruit. In America, the words jelly and jam are used interchangeably, but in Europe the definition just provided applies. For the purpose of this book we will use the European terms to refer to our jams and jellies to ensure a clear understanding of the differences between the two preserves.

When making jams and jellies you have a choice; to can them using a water bath or pressure canner, which makes them last longer, or to seal them in jars and store them in your refrigerator. Most people will mix the two, keeping a couple of jars for use over the next month or so, and canning some for longer term storage.

Most summer fruits make great jams, but make sure you test the fruit before cooking. The sweetness of fruit can vary, so you may need to

add more or less sugar to the recipe, depending on how sweet the fruit is.

When choosing fruit for jam making you should have, in an ideal world, a mix of slightly under ripe and ripe fruit. The former is usually higher in pectin but the latter has more sugar and flavor. Practically, this is very difficult to do so you use what is at hand. Overripe fruit can be used so long as it hasn't started to go bad, but be prepared to add a little bit more pectin to it.

The basic recipe for jam is to boil fruit, sugar and possibly pectin together until the jam reaches setting point. We'll go through this in more detail shortly. Some jams do not need pectin, which helps it thicken and set. Although you can make pretty much any jam without it, the jam may end up being quite runny.

Pectin – To Use or Not To Use

Pectin is a gelling agent which occurs naturally in some fruits and less in others, meaning some fruits are difficult to make a decent jam from without adding pectin.

You can buy powdered or liquid pectin, which will come with full instructions for use and quantities required. Alternatively, you can buy jam sugar which contains pectin. Note that this is different from preserving sugar, which contains other additives which reduce the scum that forms on the top of the fruit mixture.

Generally, you use ½oz (13g) per 2.2lbs (1kg) of sugar, but if the fruit only has a minor deficiency in pectin then you can safely half this otherwise your jam will set so solid you'll need a chainsaw to cut it!

Cooking apples are naturally high in pectin, so are often combined with low or medium pectin fruits when making jam, e.g. Apple and elderberry or apple and blackberry.

Fruits that are high in pectin and do not need any adding to jam are:

Blackcurrants Cooking Apples Cranberries Damsons Gooseberries Plums

Redcurrants Quince

The following fruits have medium pectin levels and can use half the recommended quantity of pectin.

Apricots (fresh – not dried) Blackberries (early) Greengage Loganberries Raspberries

These fruits have low levels of pectin and require the full quantity of pectin when making jam.

Blackberries (late) Cherries Elderberries Medlars Pears Rhubarb Strawberries

You can make your own pectin stock to use in your jam making, if you prefer, it isn't difficult to do.

1) Slice (do not peel or core) 4lb (1.8kg) of crab or cooking apples
2) Put in a saucepan, cover with water and bring to the boil

3) Simmer until the apples are mushy
4) Strain through a sieve, pushing the pulp through into a bowl
5) Cover and leave overnight
6) Return to the boil and reduce the liquid by half

This can be refrigerated for a couple of days before use. With this homemade stock you will use ½ pint for every 4 pounds of fruit for low pectin fruit and less with medium pectin level fruits.

Some people will use lemon to add pectin and to help preserve the jam, but this isn't for everyone as the lemon does add a flavor to the fruit.

Jam Making Equipment

When making jam you will need some specialist equipment. Some of this you are likely to have in your kitchen already, but other items you are unlikely to have and will need to buy.

Jam Jars

You will need clean and sterile jars to store your jam in. Although you can buy these, most people will keep glass jars they use and ask friends and family to do the same. The jars should be jam jar sized, though you can use bigger, and are best with a screw top, metal lid which is plastic coated.

The lid isn't too important as you can seal the top of jam using the traditional method of a wax disc.

Jars can be sterilized by putting them upright in your oven, with the lids next to them for about ten minutes on a low heat. This is often done whilst you are making your jam, with the oven being switched off and the door left closed to keep the jars warm.

Preserving Pan

For smaller amounts of jam, you can use any large, heavy based saucepan, but for serious jam making you will need a much larger pan. Specialist, stainless steel preserving pans are well worth buying, though they aren't cheap. They are designed for making jam and are worth buying if you are planning to make a lot of jam.

Wide Necked Funnel

You are not likely to have one of these in your kitchen, but when you have burnt your hands and spilt jam everywhere trying to get it into a jar, you will realize how valuable these are. These funnels are not expensive and will make jam making much easier, so buy one today.

Jam Thermometer

Also known as a sugar thermometer, this is very helpful to know when the setting point has been reached. These aren't strictly necessary and it is still worth using the saucer test to make sure the jam will set. A room thermometer is not suitable for measuring the high temperatures involved in jam making.

Waxed Paper Circles

When you have filled the jars, they are wiped clean and then a waxed paper disc is placed, wax side down, on top of the jam before you screw the lid on. Make sure this is flat and it will prevent mold growing. If you are using plastic coated lids these discs are not strictly necessary, but a lot of people use them anyway.

Labels

Also, very important because every jar needs labelling with not only the contents but the date too so you know which jars to use first.
You can use ornate, fancy labels or just simple white labels. It is

entirely up to you, though nice labels always means the jam can be given as a gift!

Stone Remover
If you are making jam from fruits, like cherries, with stones in the middle then a stone remover is going to make your life a lot easier!

Jelly Bag

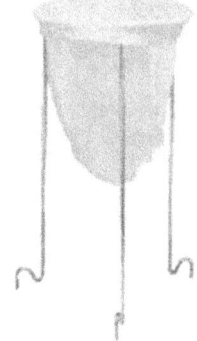

If you are making jellies and even fruit cheese (we'll talk about those later too) then a jelly bag, also known as a strainer bag, will help you strain the mixtures. Make sure you get one that comes with a stand as it makes the whole pouring process an awful lot easier.

Other Useful Items

When making jam, there are some other bits and pieces you will find useful. Some of these are likely to already be in your kitchen, such as:

Long handed wooden spoon (used for stirring)
Slotted metal spoon (used for removing scum from the top of jam)
Accurate sales Metal sieve Grater / peeler

As you make more jam you will start to build up your equipment and work out what you need. If you want to save money, look to buy these at the end of the season when they are being sold off or look online where you can make some good savings.

Fruit, Sugar, Water and Acid
The fruit you choose for your jam needs to be dry and not damaged. Over ripe fruit is lower in pectin and can be harder to set into a jam. Damaged fruit can make the jam go moldy.

When making jam, the fruit is softened by simmering, which extracts the pectin. This, when boiled with jam, makes the mixture set. If you add the sugar too early, before the fruit has cooked properly, the jam does not set correctly and the fruit skin becomes tough.

It is possible to use frozen fruit to make jam, but you will need to adjust the recipe so there is around 10% more fruit to sugar, which will make up for the pectin lost during freezing. Alternatively, you can just add more pectin!

In order for a jam to set, it needs three things:

1) Acid
2) Pectin
3) Sugar

The acid is important as it helps give the jam a better color as well as a fruitier taste rather than a sugary taste. There are some fruits which are higher in acid naturally, and others which need a bit of help by adding some acid before the cooking starts.

Fruits low in acid include:

Bilberries Blackberries (late) Blueberries Cherries
Medlars Peaches Pears Quinces Strawberries

Fruits which are high in acid include:

Apples (cooking) Blackberries (early) Blackcurrants Cranberries Damsons Gooseberries Loganberries Morello Cherries Plums Raspberries Redcurrants

The majority of recipes will tell you how much acid to use in your jam. Usually, you will use lemon juice or citric acid. Most people will use lemon juice because it is easy to get hold of and store. You can

use fresh lemons if you prefer, but bottled lemon juice does the job just as well. You need to remember that two tablespoons of lemon juice is equal to the juice of a single lemon.

If you are using citric acid then one level teaspoon of citric acid dissolved in half a teacup of water is equivalent to the juice of one lemon. You can also use tartaric acid instead of citric acid.

Sugar in Jam

You can use any sugar to make jam or even honey, if you want. Brown sugars will generally give you a darker colored jam, which can take away from the color of the fruit. Most people will use granulated white sugar for their jam as it is cheap and easy to get hold of.

You can help the sugar dissolve in the fruit by warming the sugar in an oven heated to 140C/275F for 4 or 5 minutes before adding it to the fruit. This isn't necessary, but it does make the sugar dissolve faster.

It is important that the sugar is properly dissolved in the jam before transferring to jars otherwise you will end up with a jam that is far too sugary.

Preserving sugar dissolves quickly and reduces the amount of scum that forms on the surface of the jam whilst cooking. It is more expensive than normal sugar, but for small amounts of jam it is is ideal. Some people will use normal sugar and add a few drops of glycerine which does the same job of reducing scum.

Jam sugar is different to preserving sugar and has pectin added to it to help the jam set. This is useful for low pectin fruits but for high pectin fruits jam sugar will be too much. Jam sugar is more expensive than regular sugar, so most people will use regular sugar and pectin, particularly when making larger quantities of jam.

You cannot use artificial sweeteners in jam making because although it can add sweetness, it does not preserve the fruit or help it set.

Most of the time you will use an equal amount of sugar to fruit in your jam making recipes, but this will vary depending on the pectin levels of the fruit. Low pectin fruits tend to need more sugar.

You will add water to your jam making. Juicy fruits such as strawberries, raspberries and so on will only need a little bit of water adding, which prevents the fruit burning on to the bottom of the pan. Other fruits such as rhubarb, apples, greengage and plums will need about half the volume of fruit added as water to ensure they boil properly. Tougher fruits such as quinces, pears and blackcurrants need an equal volume of fruit and water.

Citrus fruits (oranges, limes, grapefruit and lemons) need between two and three times as much water as fruit in order for them to become a jam.

If you live in an area with hard water or water that has a funny taste then it is worth filtering your water before using it in your jam to prevent the taste transferring into the final product.

Testing for Pectin

Pectin is the gelling agent that makes the jam set. Different fruits have different levels of pectin depending on the season and the fruit's ripeness. It is crucial you check pectin levels to ensure your jam sets properly. If your jam doesn't have enough pectin, then it will not set properly, so you need to know exactly how to test for it.

High pectin fruits will usually be okay, but it is worth testing anyway as it helps you determine how much more you need to simmer the fruit. Sometimes the fruit hasn't been cooked enough to extract the pectin and just needs more cooking time.

To test for pectin you will need a cup, a teaspoon and a bottle of methylated spirits.

The standard test is as follows:

1) Carefully scoop a teaspoon of the boiling fruit juice out of your saucepan and put in a cold cup
2) Leave it to cool for a minute
3) Add three teaspoons of methylated spirit, swirling the liquid around in the glass
4) If there is enough pectin, a large clot will form in the juice and you can add the sugar to the fruit mixture
5) If several small clots form then there is a medium amount of pectin and you can add some more pectin to ensure the jam sets properly

6) When there is insufficient pectin the fruit juice will break into lots of small pieces and you need to act more pectin

If you are using a high pectin fruit and the test reveals that the pectin levels are not high enough, simmer the fruit for longer, another five or ten minutes should do. This will extract more pectin energy from the fruit, allowing it to set properly.

Be aware that adding too much pectin will create a jam that is too solid and will not spread. Over time you will learn to judge the amount of pectin required by a jam, but following the instructions given will ensure your jam turns out okay.

Basic Jam and Jelly Method
We've talked a lot about the process of making jam without going into the precise method, so now we'll discuss the basic jam making method, including testing the setting point and then you will learn a variety of jam recipes.

Understanding the basic process is important because it will help you with the rest of the recipes and allow you to make your own jams and jellies out of whatever fruit you have to hand.

The basic method is as follows:

1) Wash the fruit, drain it and pat dry
2) Remove any stalks or stones as well as any damaged fruit
3) Weigh the fruit and note the weight

4)   Put the fruit into your preserving pan, then add water and acid, as required

5)   Bring to the boil, reduce to a simmer and simmer until the fruit is soft

The basic process for making a jelly is:

1)   Repeat the process for making jam, though stones and stalks can be left in place

2)   Strain through a jelly bag

3)   Re-heat the juice in your pan

Testing for Setting Point

Once the mixture has boiled for a while, determined by the recipe, you need to test for the setting point. There are three ways of doing this.

The first method is the traditional method, known as the saucer method. A teaspoon of the jam is put onto a cold saucer (taken from the refrigerator or freezer) and allowed to cool for a minute. Gently push the surface of the blob of jam with your finger. If the surface wrinkles then the jam has reached setting point, otherwise boil for longer before retesting.

A second method involves dipping a wooden spoon into your jam and removing it. Hold it for a couple of seconds with the jam on it then tip the spoon so the jam drips. The drops will run together as flakes when setting point has been reached.

The third method is the one with the least amount of chance of getting it wrong. The first two require a little experience and can take

a few attempts to get right – I'd recommend checking out a couple of videos online so you know exactly what the setting point looks like.

Dip your sugar thermometer into some hot water, give the jam a good stir and then put the thermometer into the jam, making sure the bulb does not touch the bottom of the pan. The temperature needs to be 105C / 220F in order for setting point to have been reached.

Your jam will have some scum on it which is removed using a slotted metal spoon or you can add some glycerine which will help remove it. Some people will just stir it in, but it won't always disappear and will need removing.

As soon as the setting point is reached the jam should be removed from the heat and put into clean, sterile jars, leaving a ¼" headspace. Put your wax paper circle, wax side down, on the top of the jam and wipe the jars clean. Put the lid on and seal, or cover with cellophane and an elastic band to hold the cellophane tight on the jar.

Leave the jam to cool and then label with the contents and date before storing. Once open, use a jar within two weeks.

Low Sugar Jams

Jams are naturally high in sugar, but you can make jams with less sugar if you are concerned about eating too much sugar or are diabetic.

You can use less sugar, but this does make it harder for the jam to set. Therefore, if you reduce the sugar amount you may have to increase the amount of pectin. Adding sweetener instead of sugar will sweeten the jam but it does make it much harder for it to set. If you are using sweetener in your jam, then adding more pectin can help the jam set, just be careful that the taste and consistency are okay.

Making Marmalade

Making marmalade follows similar principles to making jam, though more water is required because the rind needs longer to cook and soften. The fruit is simmered until the liquid has reduced in volume by half and the rind is soft. Marmalade is like a jam, but made from citrus fruit, including the rind and is typically slightly bitter rather than sweet, like a jam. It might sound a bit peculiar, but it is very popular in Europe and very tasty.

You can make a jelly marmalade, which is made in the same way but strained through your jelly bag and the cooked rind added afterwards.

Marmalade does tend to be more bitter than jam so you need to adjust the sugar and fruit as required to make it sweet enough for your taste. Seville oranges are a popular choice of marmalade, though they are bitter. Any citrus fruit can be used from oranges to lemons, tangerines, kumquats, satsuma, grapefruit and so on. You can use a single fruit or you can use a combination – it is up to you.

One of the lovely things about marmalade is that you can flavor it with a wide variety of ingredients such as ginger, champagne, whiskey, bourbon, brandy, rum and more. The important thing with these additional ingredients is that the citrus flavor dominates, leaving an undertone of the extra ingredient.

To make marmalade you use the same equipment as if you were making jam, though you will also need a decent sharp knife as well as a juice extractor.

Citrus fruit does contain pectin, but in the pips and the white pith. For the marmalade to set properly, it often benefits from citric acid being added as a pound of fruit will typically make about three pounds of marmalade.

The fruit needs to be washed and gently scrubbed before being fully dried. It is then sliced or shredded according to your recipe and preference. If you aren't keen on the bitter pith, which most people aren't, then you should remove the pith from the peel and put it, and the pips, in a muslin bag. Of course, you can just add pectin if you prefer. For jelly marmalade, it is best to remove the pith otherwise you end up with a bitter taste when you eat the jelly.

Thick Marmalade Recipe
This is a simple, basic recipe for making a delicious, thick cut marmalade. Use whatever fruit you want and adjust the recipe as required for your personal taste!

1) Wash, gently scrub and dry the citrus fruit
2) Peel the fruit, remove the pith and pips, putting them into a muslin bag for later
3) Put the pulp into your pan, squishing it with a wooden spoon to get some of the juice out
4) Slice the skin of the citrus fruits into a size and thickness you like
5) Using 2 to 3 times water to fruit, simmer gently in a pan with the muslin bag for two hours or until the peel has softened
6) Lift out the muslin bag, squeezing it against the side of the pan to get all the juice out of it
7) Use the saucer method to test the setting point. If it isn't setting well, add the juice of one lemon for each pound of fruit used, simmering until the setting point is reached
8) Remove from the heat, stir in the sugar until it dissolves and then return to the boil
9) Boil rapidly for between 15 and 30 minutes until the marmalade sets properly when tested
10) Skim off any scum and add some glycerine to reduce any remaining scum
11) Leave the marmalade to cool for 10-15 minutes before putting in jars otherwise the peel tends to rise to the surface
12) Pour into sterile jars, put a wax circle on, wipe the jar clean and then seal
13) Once the jars are cool, label and date the marmalade before storing in a cool, dark place

Jelly Marmalade Method

Making a jelly marmalade requires a slightly different process.

1) Wash the fruit and remove the peel, careful to get off as much pith as you can, which is put to one side
2) Cut the peel into thin strips and put in a muslin bag
3) Cut the rest of the fruit, putting it, the pith, the pips and the muslin bag into a bowl
4) Cover with water and leave soaking overnight
5) Put the mixture into a preserving pan, bring to the boil and then simmer for between 1½ and 2 hours until the peel is soft
6) After an hour remove the bag, rinse it and leave to one side to cool
7) Pour the fruit mixture into your jelly bag and allow it to strain overnight
8) Test the mixture for pectin levels
9) Measure the quantity of juice and then heat it in a pan
10) Add 1lb (454g) sugar to each pint (570ml) of juice, stirring to dissolve the sugar
11) Add extra pectin as required from your test
12) Stir in the extra peel
13) Bring to the boil and continue to boil rapidly until the setting point is reached
14) Remove any scum using a slotted spoon
15) Allow the marmalade to cool slightly to prevent the peel rising to the surface
16) Carefully pour into sterile jars

17) Wipe the jars clean and cover with either cellophane or seal with lids

18) Allow to cool before labelling and storing in a cool, dry place

Making Jam in Bread Machines & Microwaves

So far, we have discussed making jam the traditional way, but technology has advanced and you can make jam with a microwave, a bread maker or even special automatic jam making machines.

Firstly, microwave ovens. These can be used to make jam, but there are significant health and safety risks involved. Heating large volumes of liquid in a microwave is dangerous unless it is stirred often or a wooden spoon is left in it. This is because pockets of super-heated liquid can be created which can explode either in the microwave or when you take it out. On top of this, you are moving the bowl in and out of the microwave a lot, which increases the risk of dropping it or spilling it.

Making small amounts of jam in a microwave is much safer, but for many of us that is not enough jam and it is easier to make it the traditional way. You should use a bowl that is three times the size of the final jam volume, for safety purposes. When you add the sugar to the fruit the volume will double, so be aware it will take up a lot of space. However, for making small quantities of jam, the microwave method is a lot easier and requires a lot less equipment.

A basic method for microwave jam is as follows:

1) Put the fruit in a microwaveable container three times the size of the final jam volume (twice the size as a minimum)

2) Cook on full power until soft, about 4 minutes
3) Stir the sugar in until it has dissolved
4) Cook for a further 3 minutes on full power
5) Stir thoroughly
6) Repeat this process until you have cooked the jam to setting point, which will take around 18 minutes
7) Stir in some glycerine (or a small knob of butter) to remove the scum
8) Cool for 5 minutes before putting into jars and sealing

Jam Making Machines

You can buy jam making machines for your kitchen and some bread makers can be used to make jam as well as bread and cakes. Both will produce decent jams, but you need to follow the manufacturer's instructions to the letter.

The downside of these automatic machines is that it does limit your ability to experiment plus they typically make smaller amounts than you would make in a preserving pan. However, they are a quick and easy way to make jam and ideal for anyone who wants to just make small quantities without the effort of traditional jam making.

Jam & Jelly Recipes

There are a huge amount of jam and jelly recipes that you could make, and as you get used to the process you will start to create your own jam recipes, adjusting recipes such as these to your own tastes. Experimentation is a big part of the fun of jam making and you can make some really interesting flavors! Here are some of my favorite jam recipes for you to try out and enjoy.

Spiced Pear Jam

This is a lovely jam with a very interesting taste and is great if you have a pear tree in your garden and are wondering what to do with all the pears.

Ingredients:
3lbs ripe pears (cored, peeled, cut into 1" pieces) 4 cups white sugar
1 cup crushed pineapple (keep the juice) 1 lemon
1 navel orange (or substitute for whatever type is in season) Juice of 1 lemon or 2 tablespoons lemon juice
1 tablespoon fresh ginger (peeled and chopped)
¼ teaspoon ground cloves
¼ teaspoon ground nutmeg

Method:
1)   Toss the pears and lemon juice together in a mixing bowl, ensuring the pears are thoroughly coated

2) Cut the ends off the lemon and orange, then cut in half and cut lengthwise into three wedges. Remove seeds then cut into thin slices crosswise

3) Put the orange, lemon, pineapple and pineapple juice into a large pan, and simmer, stirring often, over a low to medium heat for around 20 minutes until the citrus fruit is tender

4) Add the sugar, pear, ginger and spices, and cook on a low heat, stirring often, for another two minutes until it has thickened

5) Put in jars and seal

Apricot Jam

This is a simple jam and a great use for apricots with few other ingredients.

Ingredients:

3¼ cups apricots (washed, pitted, cut into small pieces with the peel on)

7 cups sugar

½ bottle fruit pectin

Method:
1) Crush the apricots and mix with the sugar
2) Heat rapidly to a rolling boil, stirring constantly
3) Boil hard for a minute
4) Remove from heat and stir in the pectin
5) Skim, test setting point and jar when ready

Gooseberry Jam

This is probably my favorite jam. I love gooseberries, they have a wonderful flavor and this jam is delicious on toast. My favorite part is getting a piece of sweetened gooseberry on the bread ... to die for!

Ingredients:

2 quarts gooseberries
4 cups sugar
Juice of 1 lemon (or two tablespoons of lemon juice)

Method:
1) Trim both ends from the gooseberries and wash
2) Grind in a food chopper with a medium to coarse blade or chop roughly
3) Put all the ingredients into your preserving pan
4) Bring to the boil then simmer, stirring often, until setting point has been achieved

Strawberry Jam

This is a favorite with most people and eating a jam with chunks of delicious, sweet strawberry in is heaven. This is worth making with fresh, in season strawberries as the taste will be amazing.

Ingredients:
1½ pints strawberries (hulled and cut in half) 2 cups white sugar
1 large lemon (juiced and zested)

Method:
1) Mix the lemon juice and zest together with the sugar into a saucepan
2) Cook for about 10 minutes, until the sugar has dissolved, on a low heat
3) Add the strawberries, and continue to cook on a low heat for a further 20 minutes to allow the strawberries release their juices
4) The mixture will slowly start to boil and then start testing the setting point
5) When the jam sets properly, remove from heat and jar

Plum Jam
Another great recipe for anyone who has a plum tree at home as a method for dealing with the glut that happens every season.

Ingredients:
3lb firm plums (pitted and cut into 8 pieces) 7½ cups white sugar
½ cup water

3oz packet of pectin

1 tablespoon lemon juice

Method:
1) Put the plums, lemon juice and water into your preserving pan
2) Bring to the boil, stirring constantly
3) Reduce the heat, cover and simmer until soft, around 10 minutes, stirring often – the mixture should have reduced during this time
4) Add the sugar and return to a full boil stirring all the time
5) Add the pectin, return to the boil and boil for just one minute, continuously stirring
6) Remove from the heat, test the setting point
7) When the setting point has been reached, cool for a minute and skim off any scum
8) Jar, label and store

Fig Jam

This is an unusual jam and definitely worth trying. It has an unusual, but pleasant taste.

Ingredients:
12 dried black mission figs
½ cup sugar
½ cup water
½ cup hazelnuts (toasted)
3 tablespoons apple juice or brandy

Method:
1) Mix the brandy, figs, water and sugar together in a saucepan and cook on a medium heat
2) Bring to the boil, stirring often, then reduce the heat and simmer for 5 minutes, until the sugar dissolves
3) Remove from the heat, leave to cool for 10 minutes
4) Put into a food processor, add the hazelnuts and blend until smooth and thick
5) Then jar and enjoy

Grape Jelly

A popular jam in America, this is easy to make with a good quality grape juice that is delicious in a sandwich or on toast.

Ingredients:
4   cups white (granulated) sugar 3 cups grape juice
1   packet pectin
2   tablespoons lemon juice 1 teaspoon butter

Method:
1) Put the grape juice, butter, pectin and lemon juice into your preserving pan
2) Bring to a rolling boil on a high heat, stirring continuously
3) Boil for one minute
4) Stir in the sugar and keep stirring until it has dissolved
5) Return to the boil and boil for a minute, still stirring

6) Remove from heat and test the setting point

7) When the setting point has been achieved, skim scum and jar

Seville Orange Marmalade

This is a wonderful marmalade, made with a delicious orange. Depending on whether Seville oranges are available you may substitute for another large, sweet orange. The easy way to get the seeds out of an orange is to cut it horizontally, across the middle rather than from end to end.

Ingredients:

6 Seville oranges

1 naval orange

10 cups / 2½ litres water

6 cups / 1.6kg white (granulated) sugar Pinch of salt

Optional – tablespoon of whiskey or bourbon

Method:

1) Wash and dry the oranges

2) Juice the Seville oranges and remove all the seeds

3) Tie the seeds in a muslin bag and set aside

4) Cut the rind into small pieces, no more than 1/3" long (remove all the pith if you want a less bitter taste)

5) Cut the navel orange into pieces of the same size

6) Put the orange, seed bag, Seville orange juice, water and salt into a large pan

7) Bring to the boil and then simmer for between 20 and 30 minutes until the peel becomes translucent

8) Test for pectin levels - you can remove the mixture from the heat, cover and leave overnight to allow the seeds to release more pectin, though you can just add some pectin

9) Stir in the sugar and bring the pan to the boil again, reducing the heat so it boils gently, stirring often

10) After 10 to 15 minutes, remove the seed bag and discard

11) Cook until the mixture reaches 220F/140C, then test the marmalade setting point, continue cooking until setting point has been achieved

12) Remove from the heat and stir in any whiskey you are using

13) Jar, seal, label and store

Mandarin Marmalade

This is another lovely marmalade, made from the sweeter mandarins with the addition of some of your favorite whiskey to compliment the orange taste.

Ingredients:
4½lb / 2kg mandarin oranges
2lb 4oz / 1kg white (granulated) sugar 3 cups water
2 tablespoons whiskey or brandy Juice & peel of 1 lemon

Method:
1) Peel the oranges, remove the seeds and get rid of about half of the skin (you only need half for this recipe)

2) Put the oranges in your blender and blend for a couple of minutes

3) Finely slice both the lemon and mandarin peel

4) Add everything, except the whiskey, to your preserving pan and heat on a medium heat, stirring often, until the sugar dissolves

5) Increase the heat and boil for between 45 and 60 minutes, until setting point is reached – stirring occasionally

6) Taste and adjust sugar levels as required

7) Remove from the heat, stir in the whiskey

8) Jar, seal, label and store

Rhubarb Jam

Anyone who grows rhubarb will know just how much a single plant can produce in a year, making this an ideal recipe to make. The taste of rhubarb is complimented by ginger, which can be added to this recipe (to taste) to give it an even more delicious flavor. Rhubarb combines particularly well with ginger, and the addition of fresh or ground ginger to this jam can make it even more special. Unless you want chunks of ginger in your jam, I'd recommend crushing some fresh ginger, tying it in a muslin bag and then boiling the jam with the muslin bag in it.

Ingredients:

1lb rhubarb (approximately 4 stalks)

¾ cup white (granulated) sugar

½ cup water

1 teaspoon pectin

Method:

1) Trim the ends off the rhubarb and cut into ½" lengths – if the rhubarb is stringy, run a potato peeler along the length of each stalk to remove the stringy bits
2) Put the sugar, water and rhubarb into a saucepan and simmer for 10 to 20 minutes until the rhubarb breaks down. If you are adding ginger, add the muslin bag with it in at this time
3) Add the pectin and cook for a further 4 or 5 minutes, stirring often, until when you move the jam to one side you can see the bottom of the pan
4) Remove from the heat and transfer to a blender
5) Purée for about 30 seconds
6) Cool, refrigerate and enjoy

Green Tomato Jam

Often you end up with green tomatoes towards the end of the growing season. These are usually made into a chutney, fried or thrown out, but they can be made into an interesting jam!

Ingredients:

4lb green tomatoes
4 1/3 cups superfine (caster) sugar Juice & zest of 2 small lemons

Method:

1) Rinse and dry the tomatoes
2) Cut into wedges, remove the juice, seeds and the white central parts

3) Dice what is left of the tomatoes

4) Put the tomatoes, lemon juice and sugar into a bowl, cover and leave overnight

5) Pour this into your preserving pan and bring to the boil and simmer for 10 minutes, stirring regularly

6) Return to the glass bowl, cover, cool and refrigerate overnight

7) Put the mixture back into the preserving pan and boil again, skimming off any scum

8) Simmer, stirring occasionally, for a further 10 minutes

9) Check the setting point and continue to cook until setting point has been reached

10) Jar, seal, cool, label and store

Cranberry and Orange Jelly

This is a surprisingly tasty jam, with the tartness of the cranberries being offset pleasantly by the sweetness of the oranges. This is great served with holiday meals, working very well with white meat such as turkey and chicken. To give this a rounder flavor, try adding some port or replacing some or all the water with red wine.

Ingredients:

1lb fresh cranberries 5 to 10 whole cloves 1 whole star anise

Juice & zest of 2 oranges

1 to 1½ cups water (depending on how juicy the cranberries are)

¾ to 1 cup white (granulated) sugar (to taste)

¼ teaspoon ground allspice

¼ teaspoon ground cinnamon Pinch of salt

Method:

1) Put all the ingredients into a saucepan, ensuring the cranberries are covered with water

2) Bring to the boil, cover, reduce the heat and simmer for about 10 minutes (you should hear the cranberries popping during this time)

3) Reduce the heat and taste – stirring in the sugar to get your desired sweetness

4) Cook for another 5 or 10 minutes to thicken

5) Test setting point, but note it will thicken considerably on cooling

6) Serve warm or jar, refrigerate and eat later

Spiced Apple Jelly

This is a delicious jelly that has some wonderful, complimentary flavors. It will store for a year unopened, or refrigerated and kept for around 3 weeks once opened.

Ingredients:

2lb 4oz / 1kg apples – use a mixture of cookers and desert apples

1/3 cup / 75ml cider vinegar

1 cinnamon stick

12 cloves

White (granulated) sugar Water

Method:

1) Roughly chop the apple, don't core or peel

2) Put into a saucepan and cover with water
3) Stir in the spices then bring to the boil
4) Reduce the heat, cover and simmer for 45 minutes
5) Suspend your jelly bag over a large bowl
6) Pour the mixture into your jelly bag and leave to strain overnight (don't squeeze the jelly bag as it will make the final jelly cloudy)
7) Measure how much juice you have
8) Return the juice to your pan, stirring in 1lb sugar for every pint of apple juice
9) Add the cider vinegar and stir well
10) Bring to the boil, boiling rapidly for about 10 minutes until it reaches setting point
11) Jar, cover, seal, cool and label.

Orange and Cardamom Marmalade

This is quite an unusual marmalade with the cardamom giving the marmalade a pleasant tang.

Ingredients:
2½lb oranges
¾lb lemons

8 cups white (granulated) sugar 6 cups water
20 green cardamom pods (crushed)

Method:
1) The day before cooking, prepare the fruit by washing and drying both the oranges and lemons
2) Trim the stem ends and discard
3) Cut both fruits into four pieces and remove all the seeds, reserving for later use
4) Cut all the oranges and lemons into very thin slices and put into a large pot, together with any juice
5) Add the water and press the fruit down so it is under the water
6) Cover and leave for 24 hours to release pectin and soften the rind
7) The next day, bring the pot to the boil and boil steadily for half an hour
8) Wrap both the citrus seeds and the cardamom pods in a muslin bag
9) Stir in the sugar and put the cheesecloth bag into the pan
10) Continue to boil until setting point is achieved
11) Remove and squeeze out the muslin bag
12) Test the setting point
13) When set, jar and store as normal

Making Chutneys

Chutneys are very popular in the UK, having originated in India. The word derives from the Hindi word chatni, which is a savory sauce often with a tomato base. British explorers loved the taste, brought it home and now chutney are enjoyed all over the world.

Chutneys can be made from a variety of fruits and vegetables, ranging from sweet to hot to sour to mild and more. You can really personalise these to your preferences and they are great served with cold meats or cheese. Depending on the chutney it can be stirred into bolognese or other dishes to give it extra flavor. I will often use chutney when making a cheese sandwich, to give it some extra bite!

Traditional Indian Chutney

One of the advantages of making a chutney is that you use a lot of spices and vinegar, which means it doesn't matter if you are using damaged or bruised produce. Chutneys are great to use up the last of your produce such as green tomatoes, the last of your rhubarb or windfall apples. Mixed together with spices you end up with a delicious sauce that makes great use of produce that otherwise may have gone to waste.

Chutneys improve in flavor as they age as the spices and vinegar permeates the fruit and vegetables. It will take two or three months of patient waiting before you can crack open a jar and give it a taste. Open it too early and the flavor will not be as full as it could otherwise be.

Properly stored, a chutney can last for a few years because of the sheer volume of spices and vinegar that preserve the contents.
However, you should apply common sense and if it smells funny or off, you shouldn't eat it.

The equipment needed to make chutney is pretty much the same as making jam. However, you need to ensure that any metal tools you use, and that includes your preserving pan, are not reactive to the acids in the vinegar, otherwise you end up with a metallic tasting chutney.

Pans lined with enamel or made from stainless steel are fine, but cast iron, copper and aluminium should not be used as they will give your chutney a metallic taste.

You will need a long handled spoon for stirring your chutney. Be aware that if you use a wooden spoon for chutney it could absorb flavor from the vinegar and spices which could then be imparted to a jam or other dish. A long plastic spoon is better (like those used in wine making) or have a specific chutney making wooden spoon that isn't used for anything sweet.

The jars you use are very important too. Vinegar corrodes metal so if you are using any metal lids they need to be plastic coasted. I'd recommend using the Kilner style of jars with a glass lid and rubber seal, just remember to replace the seals if they start to perish.

One of the most important ingredients is the vinegar. You need good quality malt (brown) vinegar, wine vinegar or distilled malt (white) vinegar). You need an acidity level of at least 5%. If the bottle does not state the acidity level then it is less than 5% and not suitable for making chutneys that for long-term storage.

Sugar is also a key component in chutney making. White or granulated sugar can be used, as can any of the brown sugars. A brown sugar will give the chutney a darker color, which some people prefer. If you prefer a lighter color, then add the sugar when the fruit and vegetables have softened.

Spices are also used in chutney making to give flavor. Ground spices are avoided because they don't give as much flavor as whole spices plus they can give a lighter colored chutney a muddy color.
Whole or bruised spices are preferred.

The basic chutney process is pretty simple:

1) Cut your fruit and / or vegetables into even sized chunks
2) Put in a pan with vinegar, sugar and spices
3) Cook, stirring often, until the sugar dissolves
4) Simmer until the fruit/vegetables have softened and the whole mixture has thickened – there should be no runny liquid but instead of a thick, syrupy consistency
5) Jar and seal Simple, isn't it?

Chutney Recipes

Now I'm going to share with you some of my favorite chutney recipes. Remember that these will store for quite some time and when packaged nicely can make a good gift. Some people even turn chutney / jam making into a home business as people pay a premium price for high quality, hand-made products at farmer's markets and craft fairs.

Apple & Mint Chutney

This is a lovely chutney, with a bit of a bite, but goes well with most meats, particularly lamb!

Ingredients:

3lb / 1.4kg cooking apples (cored, peeled and chopped) 1lb / 450g brown Demerara sugar

1½ pints / 855ml spiced vinegar 2 red chillies (dried)

2 tablespoons fresh mint (chopped) 2 teaspoons salt

1 teaspoon whole black peppercorns

½ teaspoon whole coriander seeds

Method:

1) Slowly boil the apples and vinegar in a pan
2) Tie the spices and chillies in a muslin bag
3) Add the salt, sugar and muslin bag to the preserving pan
4) Stir as it cooks, until the sugar dissolves

5) Simmer, stirring often, until the chutney has thickened and then remove the muslin bag
6) Stir in the mint then remove from heat
7) Jar, seal, cool and label

Turnip (Rutabaga) Chutney

This is an old-fashioned chutney that is very unusual, but tasty. It works well with cold meats and is worth a try.

Ingredients:
2lb / 900g turnips (rutabaga)
1lb / 450g apples (peeled, cored and chopped) 1lb / 450g onions (peeled and chopped)
8oz / 225g sultanas 8oz / 225g sugar 1oz / 28g salt
½oz / 14g ground turmeric
1 pint / 570ml malt or spiced vinegar 1 teaspoon dry mustard powder
Pinch of cayenne pepper (or ground black pepper)

Method:
1) Peel the turnips and chop into even sized pieces
2) Boil until tender, then drain, mash and transfer to a new saucepan

3) Add the onions, apples, sugar and sultanas to the pan and stir in

4) In a separate bowl, mix together the salt, pepper, mustard and turmeric with a dash of vinegar, stirring well

5) Add this to the pan and stir in

6) Pour in the rest of the vinegar and boil, stirring occasionally

7) Reduce the heat to a simmer and cook until thickened to the desired consistency

8) Jar, seal, cool and label

Zucchini Chilli Chutney

This is a wonderful chutney and a great way to use up the glut of zucchinis (courgettes) most of us experience when we grow them ourselves. This chutney can be used straight away, though storing for a couple of weeks enhances the flavor. Adjust the amount of garlic and chillies according to your personal taste.

Ingredients:
4 medium zucchini (grated)
6 tomatoes (medium to large sized) 6-8 fresh chillies (finely seeded) 1lb 10oz white sugar
1 cup red wine vinegar Garlic bulb (minced)
1" piece of fresh ginger (grated)

Method:
1) Put all the ingredients into a pan and boil for about an hour, until the mixture thickens

2) When there is very little runny liquid then it is ready

3) Jar, seal, cool and enjoy

Onion Marmalade

A lovely recipe and one not to be confused with orange marmalade when spreading on your toast! The key to this recipe is ensuring the onions cook down well and boiling off all the moisture. When cooking the onions, choose an oil that doesn't mask their flavor, such as sunflower oil. This will last for a year in its jars, but once opened, it must be refrigerated.

Ingredients:
4½lb / 2kg onions (finely chopped)
1½ cups / 350ml distilled white vinegar 5¼oz / 150g white sugar
3½oz / 100g dark brown sugar 4 tablespoons sunflower oil 1½ teaspoons salt
½ teaspoon ground black pepper

Method:
1. Cook the onions (best done in two batches) on a low heat in two tablespoons of oil with 1 tablespoon sugar until they have reduced to a third their original size, then increase the heat and brown
2. When cooked, put all the onions and the rest of the ingredients into your preserving pan
3. Simmer until there is no loose liquid and the contents are syrupy in consistency

4. Jar, seal, cool and label

Beetroot Chutney

This is a great recipe to use with beetroot – you tend to get a lot ready to harvest at once, often too many to eat. It is a very simple recipe, but feel free to add some spices if you prefer. You can increase the amount by using equal quantities of each of the 4 main ingredients and adjusting the volume of vinegar appropriately.

Ingredients:
1lb beetroot (try mixing golden beetroot with red for more color) 1lb onions (diced)
1lb cooking apples (peel, core and chop) 1lb sugar
½ pint malt (brown) vinegar

Method:
1) Wash the beetroot and trim the leaves and roots to 1" long
2) Boil for 30 to 45 minutes, depending on the size, until a knife goes all the way through the largest beetroot
3) Drain and cool until you can handle them
4) Top and tail the beetroot, then peel and chop into ½" pieces
5) Soften the onions in a pan with some cooking oil, until they become translucent
6) Cover the onions with vinegar, then add the other ingredients
7) Continue to heat, stirring constantly until the sugar has dissolved

8) Bring to the boil and boil rapidly until the apple becomes pulpy and the whole mixture has the consistency of jam – can be anything from 20 to 60 minutes, depending on the mixture

9) Jar, seal, cool and store

Apple Chutney

This is another simple, yet tasty recipe using apples, onions and spices. Try using a mixture of cooking and eating apples to make a sweeter chutney.

Ingredients:
2lb 4oz / 1kg Bramley apples (peeled, cored and roughly chopped)
1lb 2oz / 500g onions (roughly chopped) 9oz / 250g light Muscovado sugar
3½oz / 100g sultanas
18fl oz / 500ml distilled malt vinegar 2 garlic cloves (finely chopped)
2" / 5cm piece of fresh ginger (peeled and finely chopped) 1½ teaspoons salt
Pinch of dried chilli flakes

Method:
1) Put the sultanas, apple, garlic, onion, chilli flakes and ginger into your preserving pan

2) Stir in the salt, sugar and vinegar

3) Cook on a medium heat, stirring constantly, until the sugar is completely dissolved

4) Bring the mixture to the boil, then reduce the heat and simmer for 60 minutes, stirring regularly

5) As the mixture gets thicker, stir more often so it doesn't stick to the pan

6) When you scrape a wooden spoon along the bottom of the pan and the chutney does not flow around the spoon to fill the gap, it is ready

7) Jar, seal, cool and label

Spicy Apple Squash Chutney

Squashes, and in particular, pumpkin, has a wonderful flavor when made into a chutney and this is definitely worth trying in pumpkin season. However, you can use butternut squash or other sweet, summer squashes in this recipe.

Ingredients:

2lb 4oz / 1kg pumpkin or butternut squash flesh (peeled, de- seed and cut into ½" cubes)

1lb 2oz / 500g Bramley apples (peeled and cut into ½" cubes) 1lb 2oz / 500g light brown soft sugar

3½oz / 100g fresh ginger (peeled and shredded) 1 1/3 cups / 300ml cider vinegar

15 cardamom pods (smashed) 2 large onions (finely chopped)

4 large or 6 smaller garlic cloves (peeled and thinly sliced) 2 cinnamon sticks (snapped in half)

1 large red chilli (de-seeded and finely chopped) 4 tablespoons sunflower or vegetable oil

1 tablespoon black mustard seed 2 teaspoon cumin seeds

1   teaspoon ground turmeric

Method:

1)   Heat the oil in your preserving pan on a medium heat

2)   Fry the onions, chilli, ginger, cinnamon, mustard seeds, cardamom pods and cumin seeds for around 5 minutes, stirring often, until the spices become aromatic

3)   Add the apples, squash and garlic, stir well, cooking for another 10 to 15 minutes until both the apples and onions are soft

4)   Now stir in the sugar and turmeric, simmering for another 5 minutes

5)   Add the vinegar plus two teaspoons of salt and bring to a simmer

6)   Simmer, stirring often, for about half an hour until the apple has become mushy and the pumpkin is tender

7)   When the mixture is very syrupy, but not dry (it thickens when it cools) the chutney is ready

8)   Jar, seal, cool and label

Tomato and Zucchini Chutney

This is a great chutney to use up produce that you've grown at home. The zucchini (courgette) can be your traditional green ones or you can use yellow to add some color to your chutney.

Ingredients:

2lb 4oz / 1kg zucchini (peeled, de-seeded and diced)

2lb 4oz / 1kg tomatoes (chopped) 14oz / 400g brown sugar

10½oz / 300g sultanas

2 cups / 500ml cider or white wine vinegar 4 eating apples (peeled and diced)

4 onions (chopped)

1 cinnamon stick

2 tablespoons yellow mustard seeds 1 tablespoon mixed spice

Method:

1) Put the water, vinegar, sugar and spices into your preserving pan
2) Heat, stirring often, until the sugar has dissolved
3) Add the rest of the ingredients plus a teaspoon of salt
4) Bring the pan to a simmer and cook for 2½ hours until it has thickened and looks like chutney
5) Jar, seal, cool and label

Piccalilli

This is a peculiarly British condiment based on Indian pickles. This relish is a combination of vegetables and spices, with recipes varying widely across the country. It is great in sandwiches with cheese or cold meats and is definitely worth a try if you have never had it before.

This is made from a combination of anything from 4 to 6 vegetables such as cauliflower, green beans, zucchini, tomatoes, cucumbers, carrots, shallows, peppers, tomatillos or silver skin onions. Pick vegetables you have to hand and those you like when making your piccalilli.

Ingredients:
2lb 4oz / 1kg of peeled vegetables 2½ cups / 600ml cider vinegar
5¼oz / 150g white (granulated) sugar 1¾oz / 50g honey
1¾oz / 50g table salt 1oz / 30g cornflour
½oz / 15g yellow mustard seeds
1½ tablespoons English mustard powder 1½ tablespoons ground turmeric
1 teaspoon coriander seeds (crushed) 1 teaspoon cumin seeds (crushed)

Method:
1) Wash all the vegetables and cut into even sized pieces
2) Put in a large bowl, stir in the salt and cover, leaving for 24 hours in a cool place
3) Rinse the vegetables in cold water and drain well
4) In a small bowl, mix together the mustard seeds, cumin, mustard powder, coriander, turmeric and cornflour with a little vinegar until it becomes a smooth paste
5) Pour the rest of the vinegar into your preserving pan with the sugar and honey and boil

6) Spoon out some hot vinegar and mix with the spices, stirring well
7) Put the spices into the pan and bring to the boil

8) Boil for 3 or 4 minutes so the spices release their flavors into the vinegar

9) Remove the pan from the heat

10) Add the vegetables into the sauce and fold in until thoroughly combined

11) Pack into jars and seal

12) Leave for between 4 and 6 weeks before opening and use within one year

Vegetable Soups

One of my favorite methods of storing vegetables is to turn them into soups. These are then frozen and used as and when I need them.

It is very convenient because you defrost and re-heat the soup and you have an easy meal! It is also a great way to enjoy your favorite soups all year round, even when the vegetables are not in season.

Pumpkin Soup

I grow pumpkins, potatoes, leeks and butternut squashes, all of which make delicious soups, so these are harvested and made into soups which are frozen to enjoy over the winter months. You can freeze your soups in take-away food containers (tin foil with cardboard lids) or in special thick plastic bags designed for storing soup. Either work, just remember to label the soup otherwise you end up with a bit of a lottery when you go to eat it.

When cooking your soups do not add any cream or milk products before freezing. Leave these out and add them when you are re- heating the soup. Cream doesn't freeze well in a soup and can

make it taste funny when you defrost it. I'd also recommend not putting in any fresh herbs until you are re-heating it either so you get the maximum flavor from the herbs. Fresh herbs go limp and watery when frozen and can spoil the taste of your soup.

Soup Recipes

These are some of my favorite soup recipes and I can really recommend the spicy butternut squash soup as well as the pumpkin soup – they are absolutely delicious and will be a big hit with anyone you serve them to!

Spicy Butternut Squash Soup

This is one of my favorite soups with a full flavor. It is quite easy to make, freezes well and is a very filling, thick soup.

Ingredients:

1		medium butternut squash (peeled, de-seeded and cubed) 2 carrots (peeled and chopped)
2		celery sticks (chopped)
1 large potato (peeled and cubed) 1 onion (chopped)
3 garlic cloves (crushed)
½ medium chilli (de-seeded and chopped) 2 bay leaves

Sprig of fresh rosemary
½ teaspoon chilli powder
Pinch each of cumin seeds and smoked paprika 2 pints of chicken or vegetable stock
2 tablespoons oil

Method:
1)	Heat the oil in a large saucepan
2)	Add the chilli, paprika, bay leaves, garlic, cumin seeds and rosemary, then heat for 30 seconds to release the flavor (ensure they do not start to burn or color)
3)	Add the rest of the ingredients, except the stock
4)	Cook for 2 minutes, stirring constantly, until the vegetables are covered with the spices

5) Add the stock then reduce the heat, simmering for 45 minutes until the vegetables are tender

6) Allow the soup to cool and then blend, adding more stock if required, to get your preferred consistency.

7) Reheat and serve, or freeze at this point

Potato & Leek Soup

This is another delicious, filling soup that is great to made from home-grown produce.

Ingredients:
8oz / 225g potatoes (peeled and cubed) 1 onion (peeled and sliced)
2 leeks (sliced)
2 pints / 1.2l vegetable stock 1 tablespoon vegetable oil

Method:
1) Heat the oil in a pan
2) Add the leeks, potatoes and onions and cook for around 4 minutes until they start to soften

3) Add the vegetable stock, then bring to the boil
4) Season to taste and simmer until the vegetables are tender
5) Remove from the heat and blend until you reach the desired consistency
6) Freeze or reheat and stir in 5fl oz / 150ml of double cream or crème fraiche before serving (optional)

Spicy Parsnip Soup

This is another of my favorite soups and is a great way to use up your parsnips.

Ingredients:
1½lb / 675g parsnips (peeled and diced) 2 garlic cloves (crushed)
2 plum tomatoes (quartered)
1 large onion (peeled and cut into 8 pieces) 2 pints / 1.2l vegetable stock
1 tablespoon lemon juice 1 teaspoon cumin seeds
1 teaspoon coriander seeds
½ teaspoon mustard seeds
½ teaspoon group turmeric

Method:
1) Preheat your oven to 430F / 220C or 390F / 200C for fan ovens
2) In a large bowl, mix together the spices and oil until thoroughly combined
3) Add the vegetables and stir until well coated
4) Put the vegetables on a baking sheet and roast until tender, around 30 minutes

5) Remove the vegetables from the oven and put into your blender with half the vegetable stock

6) Process until smooth

7) Return to the pan, add the rest of the stock and season to taste

8) Heat until it starts to simmer then remove from the heat and stir in the lemon juice

9) Freeze or serve garnished with cumin seeds

Pumpkin Soup

I've saved the best for last as this has to be my favorite soup of all time. Every year I get orders from friends and family for this soup and I specifically grow pie pumpkin varieties to make soup. This is definitely worth a try. This is great served topped with wild mushrooms sautéed in butter and Parmesan cheese shavings.

Ingredients:

3½lb / 1.5kg pumpkin

1 head of garlic (cut in half horizontally) 1 onion (peeled and chopped) Rosemary sprigs

Olive oil

1oz / 30g freshly grated Parmesan cheese

1.5 pints / 800ml chicken stock

3½ fl oz / 100ml double cream – stirred in just before serving Pinch of ground nutmeg

Salt and pepper

Method:
1) Preheat your oven to 340F / 170C
2) Cut the pumpkin in half horizontally and remove the seeds (tasty when roasted) and the stringy parts
3) Using a sharp knife, score the flesh of the pumpkin
4) Season with salt and pepper
5) Rub the pumpkin flesh with the garlic halves

6) In each half of pumpkin, put a garlic half and a couple of rosemary springs
7) Drizzle olive oil over this and put the pumpkin on baking trays
8) Roast for about an hour until they are tender (you can push a knife through the thickest part of the flesh without any effort when it is cooked)
9) Remove from the oven and discard the rosemary, set the garlic to one side
10) Scoop out the flesh and put into your blender, purée until smooth
11) Sauté the onion in a large saucepan until translucent, around 5 or 6 minutes
12) Scoop out the middle of 2 or 3 of the garlic cloves and add to the onion pan together with the nutmeg and some salt and pepper
13) Sauté for an additional couple of minutes
14) Add the pumpkin and the vegetable stock (if you are serving immediately add the Parmesan now, but if you are freezing then add it during the reheating)
15) Bring the pan to the boil, reduce the heat and simmer for about 10 minutes

16) If you are serving immediately, stir in the cream, but if you are freezing add it when reheating, and cook for another minute

17) Blend the soup until smooth and then freeze or reheat to serve

Fruit Leathers

Fruit leathers are a great way to preserve a wide range of fruits. A variation on dehydrating and an alternative to canning or making jam, it is a great way to preserve fruit for later in the year. This beef jerky of the fruit world is a convenient, high energy snack loved by kids and adults alike.

This is one method for making fruit leather and it will vary according the fruit you use. Use a variety of different fruits or a single fruit, it is up to you plus you can spice the fruit leather with your favorite flavorings such as nutmeg, ginger or cinnamon.

A variety of fruit leathers

This method will take about 20 minutes to prepare and approximately 9 hours to cook.

Ingredients:
Fresh fruit, e.g. Peaches, apples, apricots, plums, grapes, berries, pears
Water
Sugar, as required depending on sweetness of fruit Lemon juice

Method:
1)   Rinse and prepare the fruit, removing any stones or damaged parts, peel and core apples and pears

2) Taste the fruit to determine how sweet it is and whether you need to add any sugar

3) Measure the fruit, then add to a saucepan with ½ cup of water for every 4 cups of chopped fruit

4) Add sugar to taste

5) Simmer, covered, for 10 to 15 minutes, until the fruit is cooked throughout

6) Uncover, stir well and mash the fruit using a potato masher

7) Add lemon juice to taste, better too little than too much, this brings out the flavor of the fruit, prevents browning and helps with preservation

8) Adjust the sugar as required and add any spices you want to use

9) Return to the heat, simmer for another 5 to 10 minutes, until the sugar has dissolved completely

10) Once the sugar has dissolved, remove the mixture from the heat and purée it

11) Pour the purée onto a baking sheet (lined with plastic wrap or grease proof paper) so it is between an eighth and a quarter of an inch thick

12) Either dry in an oven (at 140F) for between 8 to 12 hours on a very low heat, careful that any plastic wrap doesn't touch the oven and melt or use a dehydrator to dry. An alternative is to leave it in the sun under cheesecloth for the day which will dry it out too

13) The leather is ready when it isn't sticky and the surface is smooth

14) Either cut the fruit leather or roll it up in the plastic wrap for a fruit roll

15) Store in an airtight container in your refrigerator or alternatively freeze it

The big advantage of this is that you can mix sweeter fruits with less sweet fruits which can reduce or even eliminate the need for adding sugar. This make the fruit leathers better for children and diabetics. Alternatively, you can use artificial sweeteners, but be aware that they can lose sweetness during drying. You can even substitute honey for sugar, which allows the fruit leathers to be stored for longer.

Remember to ensure the leather is thoroughly dry before storage otherwise it will encourage mold to grow.

The following list provides details of which fruits are suitable for use as fruit leather and which are not. This isn't a complete list, but

contains the most commonly used fruits.

Apples – perfect Apricots – excellent Avocados – not suitable
Bananas – reasonable – best as a secondary ingredient Berries with seeds – perfect
Blueberries – do not work by themselves, but great as a secondary ingredient
Cherries – perfect
Citrus fruits / peel – only use as a secondary ingredient Cranberries – only use as a secondary ingredient Grapes – reasonable

Melons – not suitable Nectarines – perfect Peaches – perfect Pears – perfect Pineapples – perfect

Plums – good, though benefit from additional ingredients Strawberries – perfect

Fruit Leathers from Frozen or Canned Fruit

If you want to make fruit leather out of certain fruits that are out of season then you can use frozen or canned fruit, which could be home-made or store-bought. Applesauce, for example, is ideal to mix in with fruits that aren't sweet or particularly good when turned into fruit leather. This sweetens the fruit and helps some fruit set as well as bulking out fruit you do not have much of.

The method is very simple, you drain the fruit and put the liquid to one side. A pint of fruit will make a 13" by 15" fruit leather. The frozen/canned fruit is puréed until it becomes smooth, but if it is too thick add some liquid, e.g. Applesauce or fruit juice, which makes the consistency better for pouring.

If the fruit is light colored, then add two teaspoons of lemon juice for every two cups of fruit. This will help the fruit retain its color and prevent oxidation which darkens it.

Spices and Flavors

Fruit leathers are delicious just by themselves, but you can make them even more interesting by adding spices to them. This can make the leathers irresistible and much more appealing to people.

Some spices you can try in your fruit leather are:

Allspice Cinnamon Cloves Coriander Ginger Mace Mint Nutmeg Pumpkin pie spice (mixed spices)

Don't over do it with the spices. Start by adding a little and then slowly increase it, tasting often so you get just the right amount of spices. I'd recommend starting with about an eighth of a teaspoon of spice for every two cups of fruit purée.

You can also add some flavorings. Again, start with a little, tasting and adding until it tastes right to you. Start with the same amount as with spices and build it up gradually.

Some flavorings you can add to your fruit leathers are:

Almond extract Citrus peel (any) Citrus juice (any) Vanilla extract

Drying the Fruit Leather

I want to talk a little bit more about drying the fruit leather as this is one of the most important steps, but also the one where people often make mistakes. Fruit leather dries from the outside to the middle. You are drying it until it has no sticky spots – you'll be able to see them – and it is still pliable. Whilst it is warm you remove the leather from the plastic wrap and either roll it up or cut it into strips, before leaving it to cool.

A dehydrator does make it much easier to dry the fruit leather. It's a lot more convenient because you aren't tying your oven up and it can be used for cooking rather than just drying. You can leave your fruit

leather drying overnight whilst there is no need to use the oven, but the downside of this is that you cannot keep an eye on it and it can dry out.

In a dehydrator, you can expect your fruit leather to take anywhere from six to eight hours to dry properly. Make sure you follow the manufacturer's instructions for use and times vary between the different dehydrators. If you are going to make a lot of fruit leather, then invest in a dehydrator as it will save a lot of time.

Oven drying is slower than a dehydrator, but it will work. Drying in the oven can take anything from eight to eighteen hours, depending on the fruits you have used, so you can see why it can be inconvenient!

If you have a fan oven, then the drying times will be reduced compared to a non-fan oven. You will set the oven to 140F / 60C for drying fruit leathers. Not all ovens will go this low, so yours may not be suitable for drying fruit leather. If your oven does not go this low, then rather than drying the fruit leather it will cook it so that it becomes inedible. The other downside of an oven is it is not as energy efficient as a dehydrator.

One way to help the drying process along is to prop the oven door open a couple of inches. This allows the evaporated water from the fruit leather to escape the oven, which helps it to dry quicker. If you have pets or small children, then you need to be very careful doing this as their inquisitive nature will mean they open the oven. If you

are leaving the oven door open, then put a thermometer in the oven as the temperature will not be steady at 140F. You may need to turn the heat up for the oven to stay at a steady temperature.

When properly dried and stored, in airtight containers, a fruit leather will keep for between two and four weeks at room temperature.
Remember to store it somewhere cool and dark though. You can freeze fruit leather where it will store for up to a year. However, in my experience with fruit leather, you are lucky if your fruit leather lasts two weeks as everyone eats it!

What I really like about fruit leather is that it is a great way to use up excess fruit. You can mix together left over fruits, so your wastage is reduced. You can even use left-over pulp from jam making and other preserving techniques. The leathers are really tasty and very popular with children, making an ideal healthy addition to a school lunchbox. They are not a lot of work to make, and if you have a dehydrator then they are even easier. I'd recommend trying some as they are delicious.

Fruit Butters & Cheeses

You may or may not have heard of fruit butters and cheeses. They are old-fashioned names used to describe a preserve made from sugar and puréed fruit, which were popular during the Middle Ages and are less popular today. Butters and cheeses are best made from fruits that are good for jellies, plus you can make them from the pulp that is left over after straining fruit through a jelly bag! This is a great way to reduce waste and use up something that may have otherwise just been thrown away.

The equipment you need to make fruit cheeses and butters is the same as you need for jam making. One additional item you will need is a plastic or fine nylon sieve.

Fruit butters are ideal for dealing with a glut of either home grown or wild fruits. They are soft and spreadable, requiring less sugar.
However, they don't store for too long because of their low sugar content. Typically, they will store for a few weeks and on opening, require refrigerating and using up in a few days.

Fruit cheeses are great for any fruit that has stones or pips, using more sugar than a fruit butter. They are made from a stiff fruit purée, being solid, like cheese. They are cut with a knife and served with poultry or cold meat. They can be eaten by themselves or on crackers. A fruit cheese will typically store for four months and improves in flavor if allowed to mature for a couple of months before using.

How to Make Fruit Cheeses and Butters

Making fruit cheeses and butters are not particularly difficult to make. The basic process is as follows, though there will be some detailed recipes towards the end of this chapter.

1) Clean and chop larger fruits, small fruits can be used whole. Discard bruised and diseased parts of the fruits

2) Put the fruit into your preserving pan and cover with cold water

3) Simmer until the fruit has softened, adding lemon juice to any fruits that are low in acid to help preserve them

4) Put the fruit, once softened, into your plastic sieve and rub it through so it produces a very fine pulp

5) Weigh this pulp and then put it into a clean pan

6) Fruit Cheese – add the same weight of sugar as there is pulp, stir until dissolved then simmer for an hour, stirring very regularly, until the cheese has thickened

7) Fruit Butter – boil the fruit pulp until it has thickened, then add half the pulp's weight in sugar plus any spices you like, before continuing to simmer until the mixture becomes creamy and thick

8) A fruit cheese is ready when you can draw a spoon across the bottom of the pan and it leaves a clean line

9) A fruit butter is ready when the surface is creamy and there is no free liquid visible

10) Fruit butters are jarred in exactly the same way as a jam

11) Fruit cheeses need to be stored in wide neck jars or molds, but they must be greased with glycerine first to stop the cheese from sticking

As always, you wipe the jars clean and cover them whilst they are still hot. Once they have cooled, then you can label the jars with both the contents and the date.

Fruit Cheese and Butter Recipes

There are lots of different fruit cheese and butter recipes, but here are some of my favorites to make that I hope you will enjoy too.

Gooseberry Butter

This is a very tasty fruit butter, with the tang of the gooseberries being offset nicely by the sugar. This is particularly nice on toast, crumpets or other bread products. It also makes a great filling for pies and cakes! In this recipe, you use ¾lb of sugar for each pound of fruit pulp, but you can adjust it according to your personal preferences. This will store for a few months but should be refrigerated and used within a week once opened.

Ingredients:
4lb / 1.8kg ripe gooseberries (topped, tailed and washed)
¾ pint / 400ml water
Sugar as required for the weight of pulp

Method:
1) Put the fruit in your preserving pan with the water
2) Boil, then simmer until the fruit is soft
3) Strain the fruit and liquid through a fine sieve into a bowl
4) Weigh the pulp

5)   Add ¾ pound of sugar to each pound of pulp (340g sugar to each 450g pulp)

6)   Put the pulp back in your preserving pan and simmer

7)   Add the sugar and stir well until it is fully dissolved

8)   Continue to simmer until the mixture becomes thick and creamy

9)   Jar, seal, cool and label

Blackcurrant Fruit Butter

A lovely fruit butter, great on toast or used in pies and cakes. Like the previous recipe, this stores for a few months and should be refrigerated and used within a week once opened. Allow ¾lb (340g) of sugar for every 1lb (450g) of fruit pulp.

Ingredients:
4lb /1.8kg blackcurrants (washed) 3 pints / 1.7l water
Sugar

Method:

1)   Put the fruit in a large saucepan together with the water

2)   Bring to the boil, then reduce the heat and simmer until the currants are very soft

3)   Push both the fruit and liquid through a fine sieve into a bowl

4)   Weigh the pulp, then put it back into your pan

5)   Simmer until the mixture has thickened and reduced by around a third

6)   Add the sugar (3/4lb per 1lb of pulp) and stir well until dissolved

7) Simmer until you get the right consistency
8) Jar, seal, cool and label

Damson Cheese

This is a great recipe for damsons, though you can use it for any fruit that has pips or stones, such as plums. This will store for a few months and should be refrigerated once opened and used within a week. In this fruit cheese recipe, you allow an equal weight of sugar to fruit pulp, i.e. One pound of sugar per pound of pulp.

Ingredients:
6lb / 2.8kg damsons (washed)
½ pint / 300ml water
2 teaspoons ground allspice Sugar

Method:
1) Put the damsons in your preserving pan with the water
2) Bring to the boil then reduce the heat, cover and simmer until the damsons are soft and tender
3) Pour the mixture, including the liquid, through a sieve into a bowl, pressing through with a wooden spoon
4) Measure the purée then return it to the pan
5) Add the sugar (1lb for each 1lb of pulp) and ground allspice
6) Continue to simmer, stirring often until the sugar has completely dissolved
7) Bring to the boil, then reduce the heat
8) Cook, stirring often, until the mixture is very thick

9)   Pour into molds, cover/seal and store

Cranberry Cheese

This is a lovely fruit cheese as the tartness of the cranberries is balanced very well by the sugar. This will store for a few months but should be refrigerated and used within a week once opened.

Ingredients:
6lb / 2.8kg cranberries (washed) 6lb / 2.7kg sugar
1¾ pints / 1 litre water Juice and zest of 1 orange 1 tablespoon lemon juice
1   teaspoons ground cinnamon

Method:
1)   Put the cranberries into your preserving pan together with enough water to cover them
2)   Bring to the boil before reducing the heat, covering and simmering
3)   Stir regularly and squash the cranberries with the back of a wooden spoon
4)   Continue simmering until the fruit is very soft
5)   Pour the mixture through a sieve into a bowl, pressing through with the back of a wooden spoon
6)   Put the purée back into the pan and boil it for a few minutes if it has too much liquid so it reduces a little
7)   Add the sugar and simmer, stirring often, until the sugar has dissolved

8) Add the rest of the ingredients and stir in

9) Bring to the boil, reduce the heat and simmer until the mixture is reasonably stiff

10) Pour into molds, cover/seal and cool

Spicy Apple Butter

This is a firm favorite with anyone who tries it and is a great use of either windfall apples or crab apples. Use ¾lb (340g) of sugar for every 1lb (450g) of fruit pulp. Again, this will store for a few months, but once opened, is best used within a week and stored in your refrigerator.

Ingredients:
6lb / 2.8kg windfall apples (or crab apples) 2 pints dry cider
2   pints water Sugar
1 teaspoon each of ground clove and cinnamon
½ teaspoon ground allspice Finely grated zest of ½ lemon

Method:
1) Wash the apples, removing any bruised parts and roughly chop (coring and peeling are not necessary)

2) Put the apples into your preserving pan, together with the cider and water

3) Bring to the boil, reduce the heat and simmer until the apples are very squishy

4) Push the fruit and liquid through your sieve, weigh the pulp and return it to the pan

5) Add sugar to the pan at a ratio of ¾lb sugar for each pound of pulp

6) Continue to heat, stirring often, until the sugar has dissolved

7) Simmer until the mixture has reduced by approximately a third and has thickened up

8) Add the spices and lemon zest

9) Return to the boil, stirring often until there is no liquid left

10) Jar, seal, cool and label

Fruit Curds

Strictly speaking, fruit curds are not a preserve, but you will find them (usually lemon curd) in a supermarket on the same shelf as the jam. They are very nice, great on bread or toast, used in cakes or a filling for tarts.

Lemon Curd

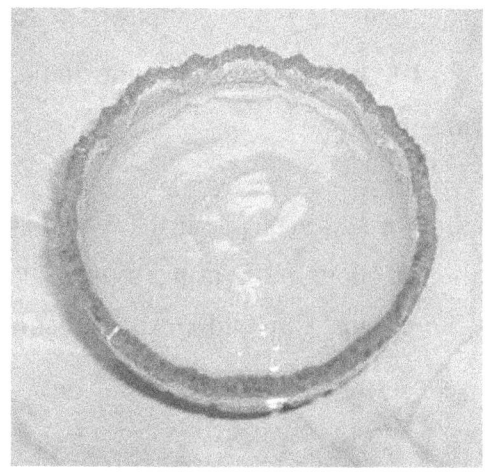

Most curds have lightly cooked eggs in them. This means that younger children, the elderly and pregnant women need to be careful as there is a small risk of salmonella. This is the same for any product with uncooked or lightly cooked eggs in them.

When making a fruit curd you also use butter. An unsalted butter is best because the salt in salted butter, though not significant, is enough to impart a flavor to your fruit curd. This flavour can be unpleasant and the slightly salty taste doesn't work well with the sweetness of the curd.

A fruit curd does not set like a jam, but it does get thicker as it cools. At the end of the cooking, the curd may be a little runny, but it will thicken up into a gooey paste as it cools. If, after cooking, the curd is too thin, you can add another egg yolk and cook for a further five to ten minutes to thicken up.

Not only does the curd thicken when it cools, but it also shrinks. When filling the jars, you need to fill right to the rim, not leaving any headspace. As the curd cools, it will shrink down and create the required headspace in the jar.

The most common fruit curd is lemon curd, though you can use any citrus fruit. Other fruits can work, such as quince, apricots, cooking apples and gooseberries. You will find lemon curd in most supermarkets, particularly in the UK, though the more unusual curds can sometimes be found in farm shops.

You will need the same equipment for making fruit curd as you do with jam. You will need a double boiler, though a heatproof bowl over a saucepan of hot water will do the job just fine and is what most of us use.

Once made, a fruit curd will store for around six weeks if kept in a cool, dark place. Storing in a refrigerator will extend the storage time to around three months. Once opened, they must be refrigerated and used within a week.

Fruit Curd Recipes

Making a fruit curd is not too difficult and once you've tried one, you will love them! If you are not sure if they are for you, buy a jar of lemon curd from the supermarket and try it. It's great on toast and wonderful as a pie filling!

Lemon Curd

This is the most common of the fruit curds and is great for a wide variety of uses, though my favorite is to eat it on toast.

Ingredients:

Juice and zest of 4 unwaxed lemons 7oz / 200g fine (caster) sugar
3½oz / 100g unsalted butter (cut into cubes) 3 eggs
1 egg yolk

Method:

1) Put the sugar, butter and lemon zest/juice into a heatproof bowl and place over a pan of simmering water (make sure the water does not touch the bowl)
2) Stir regularly, and heat until the butter has melted
3) In a separate bowl, whisk together the eggs and egg yolk before stirring them into the lemon mixture

4) Stirring occasionally, cook in the double boiler until it has become creamy and thick enough that it coats the back of the spoon, which will take between 10 to 15 minutes

5) Remove the curd from the heat and cool, stirring occasionally
6) Once cooled, put into jars and seal, storing in your refrigerator

Passion Fruit Curd

This is an unusual curd but surprisingly tasty. The passion fruit really works well in this form and you will enjoy it. This will keep for about a week in the refrigerator and is fantastic on scones, crumpets or toast!

Ingredients:
7oz / 200g passion fruit pulp (6 to 8 passion fruits should be enough)
9oz / 250g golden caster (fine) sugar 5oz / 140g unsalted butter (diced)
3 large eggs
2 tablespoons cornflower

Method:
1) Whizz the pulp in your food processor to separate the seeds from the juicy parts
2) Pour through a sieve, scraping through as much pulp as you can, leaving the seeds behind, put 2 tablespoons of the seeds to one side
3) Put everything, except the reserved seeds, into a saucepan and heat on a low heat
4) Stir constantly, until the butter has melted, do not turn the heat up as you will curdle the eggs

5)   Keep stirring constantly until the mixture has thickened and looks like lemon curd

6)   Sieve this into a clean bowl, leaving behind any pieces of curdled egg

7)   Stir in the 2 tablespoons of seeds and leave to cool

8)   Put into jars, seal and refrigerate

Grapefruit & Orange Curd

This is another unusual curd and worth a try. This one will store, if sealed properly, for up to three months in a cool, dark place and should be refrigerated once opened.

Ingredients:
1 cup / 200g superfine (caster) sugar
8 tablespoons / 115g unsalted butter (diced) 2 large eggs (beaten)
2 large egg yolks
Grated rind and juice of 1 orange
Grated rind and juice of a small red grapefruit

Method:
1)   Put both the rinds and juice in a heatproof bowl with the sugar and butter

2)   Use the double boiler method to melt the butter and dissolve the sugar, stirring often

3)   Add all the eggs to the bowl by straining them through a sieve

4)   Whisk the mixture together and continue to heat, stirring constantly, until it thickens and looks like lemon curd

5) Remove from heat and transfer to warm, sterile jars

6) Seal, cool and label before storing in a cool dark place

Cranberry Curd

Another great curd that is well worth trying. A good use for leftover cranberries after making cranberry jam for Thanksgiving.

Ingredients:

½lb fresh cranberries

¾ cup granulated (white) sugar

½ cup water 3 egg yolks

4 tablespoons unsalted butter (cubed) 1 whole egg

Method:

1) Heat the cranberries and water in a small pan (covered) over a medium heat

2) Cook until you hear the cranberries pop and the liquid starts to bubble

3) Remove from heat and push the cranberries through a strainer into a bowl, scrapping all the purée off the bottom of the strainer

4) Return the purée to the pan and put to one side

5) In a separate bowl, whisk the eggs and egg yolk until well combined

6) During the whisking process, add the sugar and continue to whisk until the mixture turns a light yellow color

7) Add the eggs to the purée and continue to whisk for another minute until well combined

8) Heat on a medium heat, stirring constantly, for 8 to 10 minutes until it thickens into a curd like texture

9) Remove from the heat and stir in the butter, a little at a time

10) Strain one more time before putting in a jar and refrigerating

Blueberry Curd

This is another great curd that is lovely on toast, crumpets or scones. This will store in your refrigerator for up to two weeks.

Ingredients:

2 cups blueberries (can be fresh or frozen) 1 cup sugar

¼ cup unsalted butter (cubed) 2 eggs (beaten)

1 tablespoon water 1 teaspoon lime zest

Method:

1) Put the berries and water into a saucepan and cook on a low to medium heat, stirring often, until the berries release their juice and the mixture boils

2) Strain the mixture into a bowl, keeping the juice and discarding the pulp from the berries (you should have about ¾ cup of juice)

3) Put the eggs, lime zest, sugar and blueberry juice in a double boiler and whisk constantly

4) Add the butter a little a time, stirring well, adding more only when the butter has melted

5) Keep stirring as it cooks until the mixture achieves a lemon curd consistency

6) Remove from heat (strain again if necessary) and jar

Ketchups & Sauces

These are another great way for you to preserve fresh produce. These are quite similar, though ketchup, or catsup as it is sometimes known, is usually slightly thinner than a sauce.

Sauces are usually rubbed through a fine mesh sieve so that the resulting mixture is smooth. Then it is cooked again to thicken so that the ingredients do not separate out but the mixture will still pour. A ketchup is often strained through a jelly bag, as used in jam making, to create a smooth purée which is then bottled.

Both ketchups and sauces are made from very similar ingredients to those used in chutney recipes, and the method is also very similar.
You will not need any special ingredients when making ketchups and sauces, but you will want to use glass bottles for storage. These can be hard to get hold of and often people will recycle plastic bottles from their kitchen cupboards or use the continental lager (beer)

bottles that have a plastic cork in a metal frame. These can be found in wine making shops or online.

When you are making sauces that have a low acid content, such as ripe tomatoes or mushrooms you need to sterilize your sauce bottles. This can be done using a water bath canner, in a dishwasher or in your oven. To effectively kill off potentially harmful organisms, you need the water temperature in your canner to be 77C / 160F for 30 minutes. A sugar thermometer is the easiest way to measure this temperature. When using bottles, rather than jars, it is better to slightly loosen the lids whilst they are in the water.
Remove them from the hot water and then allow them to cool fully before tightening the lids completely.

Depending on the bottles you are using, you may use corks to seal them. Be aware that corks are not airtight and you will need an additional seal to keep the air out and your sauce safe. I'd recommend using the plastic sleeves used in wine making which seal tight when heated with a hair dryer. These are available from any wine making store or online

Ketchup & Sauce Recipes
Here are some of my favorite sauce recipes for you to try. These are all great ways of using up excess produce and making delicious sauces too.

Gooseberry Ketchup
This is an unusual ketchup but is remarkably tasty. Gooseberries have a very unique flavor which is brought out in this recipe. Use this ketchup

with any strong meat such as duck, game birds or even venison. However, it is still fantastic with any other meat and surprisingly nice on the good old hamburger!

Ingredients:
2lb / 900g gooseberries (best is they are slightly under ripe) 12oz / 340g brown Demerara sugar
4oz / 112g sultanas
1½ pints / 860ml white wine vinegar 3 garlic cloves (crushed)
1 tablespoon mustard seeds 1 tablespoon salt
1 teaspoon cayenne pepper

Method:
1) Cut the gooseberries in half
2) Put them into a saucepan and crush them with a wooden spoon or potato masher
3) Add the rest of the ingredients to the gooseberries
4) Boil, stirring constantly until the sugar has dissolved
5) Reduce the heat, cover and simmer for about 30 minutes until the gooseberries are very soft
6) Strain through a fine mesh sieve
7) Pour into hot, sterilized bottles and seal, labelling when cooled

Simple Tomato Sauce

This is a favorite with many people and particularly popular with children. This is a very easy recipe to follow, though feel free to adjust the spices according to your personal tastes. This will keep for up to a month in your refrigerator unless you freeze or sterilize the filled bottles.

Ingredients:

6lb / 2.8kg red tomatoes (ripe)

8oz / 225g white (granulated) sugar

½ pint / 285ml distilled white vinegar 1 tablespoon salt

2   teaspoons paprika

1 teaspoon celery salt Pinch of cayenne pepper

Method:
1)   Wash and chop the tomatoes
2)   Cook slowly in a pan, stirring regularly, until they turn into a pulp
3)   Press through a sieve into a bowl, discarding the skin and seeds
4)   Return the purée to your pan, adding the rest of the ingredients
5)   Heat, stirring constantly, until the sugar is completely dissolved
6)   Bring the mixture to the boil
7)   Reduce the heat, simmering until the sauce has thickened
8)   Transfer to hot, sterilized bottles and seal, sterilize once sealed for longer storage

Horseradish Sauce

This is a great sauce with a bit of a kick, easily made from the horseradish root. The sauce itself is quite a lot of work to make for something that will only store for a day or maybe two at most. One word of warning is that horseradish is not a vegetable to be toyed with. You think onions make your eyes water … try peeling horseradish and you'll think you've been maced. Wash the root well, peel it under water and then roughly chop it before throwing it into your mincer or food processor! Avoid touching your eyes, mouth or nose after peeling this until you have washed your hands well. In fact, I'd recommend you wear gloves whilst preparing this vegetable just to be on the safe side.

Ingredients:
Grated horseradish roots (fresh) 8oz / 225g granulated (white) sugar
½ pint / 285ml distilled white vinegar 1 teaspoon salt

Method:
1)   Put the vinegar and sugar into a saucepan
2)   Heat over a low heat, stirring often, until the sugar has dissolved
3)   Remove from the heat and leave to cool
4)   Put the grated horseradish into the jar, pushing it down so it is firmly packed
5)   Pour the vinegar mixture over it until the jar is full
6)   Push down the horseradish, tap the jar to remove air bubbles and add more horseradish if necessary
7)   Seal, label and store in a cool, dark place
8)   When serving, remove what is needed from the jar and put into a small bowl. Season with salt, pepper and mustard powder to taste and add double cream, whisking until you get a smooth consistency

Spicy Tomato Sauce

This is a nice variation on the normal tomato sauce that has a bit of a kick behind it. This works well in any Italian style dish or as a dipping sauce. Without additional sterilizing, this will only store for 2 or 3 weeks in your refrigerator.

Ingredients:

3lb / 1.4kg ripe tomatoes (chopped) 8oz / 225g onion (finely chopped)

3oz / 84g white (granulated sugar)

½ pint / 290ml distilled white vinegar 10-12 black peppercorns (crushed) 2 cloves

1   bay leaf

2   teaspoons chilli powder 2 teaspoons salt

2 teaspoons paprika

1 teaspoon cayenne pepper

Method:

1)   Put the tomatoes, onions, vinegar, bay leaf, cloves, salt and crushed peppercorns into a saucepan

2)   Simmer, stirring occasionally, until thoroughly cooked through

3)   Push through a fine mesh sieve, leaving the whole cloves, peppercorns and onions out, but getting as much tomato through as you can (though not the skin or pips)

4)   Return the liquid to the pan and boil until thickened

5)   Add the rest of the ingredients and stir until the sugar has completely dissolved

6)   Taste, adjust seasoning and sugar as needed and then bottle

Chilli Sauce

This is a fabulous recipe for anyone who grows their own chillies. This is particularly good to make and throw in some of the seriously

hot peppers you can grow at home to make a wicked chilli sauce. Remember to wear gloves when handling the chillies and be careful not to get the juice on your skin or anywhere else, particularly when using the hotter peppers. Chilli sauce also has a habit of separating out in storage, so give it a good shake before using.

Ingredients:
6oz / 170g chilli peppers (any type, any mixture of hotness) 6oz / 170g onion (finely chopped)
4oz / 112g cooking apple (peeled, cored and chopped)
¼ pint / 145ml distilled white vinegar 2 teaspoons mustard powder
1 teaspoon salt

Method:
1) De-stalk and de-seed the chillies, chopping very finely – be careful not to touch your eyes, nose or mouth during this (leave the seeds in for extra heat)
2) Put the chillies in a saucepan with the rest of the ingredients
3) Heat gently, stirring often, until the mixture starts to boil
4) Reduce the heat and simmer for approximately 40 minutes until everything has softened and the sauce has thickened
5) Sieve out all the lumps and put into a hot, sterilized bottle and seal

Thai Sweet Chilli Sauce

This is a fantastic recipe to make and produces a lovely sweet, chilli sauce. Although you can use the very hottest chillies in this sauce,

I'd recommend using milder chillies so that you can enjoy the flavor of the sauce. It is great for dipping or using in your cooking. You can leave the chilli seeds in the recipe or remove them to make the sauce slightly milder.

Ingredients:
4oz / 114g sultanas (chopped) 2oz / 57g fresh chillies (chopped) 1 cup distilled white vinegar
¾ cup white (granulated) sugar
1 or 2 garlic cloves (finely chopped)
2 teaspoons fresh ginger (finely chopped)
½ to 1 teaspoon of salt (depending on taste)

Method:
1) Put the chillies and half the vinegar into your food processor and finely chop
2) Transfer this to a saucepan and add the rest of the ingredients
3) Simmer on a low heat, stirring so the sugar dissolves
4) Bring to the boil, then immediately reduce the heat
5) Simmer for another 20 minutes until both the sultanas and the chillies have softened
6) Purée until virtually smooth and then bottle

Fruit Cordials & Syrups

Cordials are an excellent way to preserve fruits, particularly wild fruits such as rose hips, elderberries, elderflowers and more.

Elderflower cordial is a wonderful, refreshing summer drink, great with lemonade or, for the grownups, white wine. Elderberry cordial is a lovely winter warmer, fantastic for colds and flu or served warm whilst watching the snow fall.

However, there are many more cordials you can make using anything from apples to pears to blackcurrants, so use up the excess fruit you have to make some delicious cordials. You need to ensure that the fruit you are using has a strong enough taste so that when you have boiled it with sugar it still tastes of the fruit, rather than just of sugar. This is the reason why you never see an apple cordial, but you will see apple and elderberry or apple and blackcurrant, because the secondary ingredient makes the cordial taste of something other than sugar.

The nice thing about home-made cordials is you are in control of the sugar in them. You can adjust the sugar levels to your preference or even use a mixture of sugar and artificial sweeteners, making these ideal for anyone who is diabetic or concerned about their (or their kids) sugar intake.

You will need bottles with clip top lids, European lager bottles are ideal and easily available online or from your local wine making store. However, you can use any bottles and either cork them yourself or seal them with a screw top lid. If you are reusing bottles then make sure they are thoroughly sterilized and cleaned so that no odor or taste remains from the previous occupant. Remember to clean the lids too as they often retain smell or taste.

You are also going to need a large saucepan, though your preserving pan is ideal for this job. A long handled wooden spoon will be needed, as will some jelly or muslin bags for straining the cordials. A good bottle brush is very useful for cleaning out the bottles too.

The basic process of making a fruit cordial is simple. Fruit is boiled down with a little water which creates a clear liquid. Then, once the liquid is strained off, sugar is added and it is heated some more. A good cordial will last up to a year if stored correctly in airtight, sterile jars.

With all the recipes to follow you need to adjust the quantities of sugar and water to reflect the amount of fruit you have. You may end up with more or less fruit than the recipe states, depending on what is available or left over. If you find a tree with three pounds of fruit on but you need four for the recipe, you're not going to throw the fruit away!

You will learn a basic procedure for making cordials and then some recipes will follow afterwards. In these recipes, remember, you are aiming for a fruity flavor rather than a sugary flavor so you may need to reduce or increase the amount of sugar depending on how sweet

the fruits are. You can use honey instead of sugar, which will give the fruit a sharper taste.

If you are picking fruit from the wild you will want to spread it out somewhere and leave it for an hour or two so that insects can leave the fruit. Flowers and fruit can have a wide variety of insects on that you probably don't want in your cordial.

The basic cordial making process is as follows, though elderflower cordial follows a slightly different procedure.

1) Wash the fruit, removing any stems, damaged parts, insects (oh yes, that does happen) and diseased fruit
2) Put the fruit into your preserving pan with ¼ pint of water for each pound of fruit
3) Bring to the boil, reduce the heat and simmer until the skin of the fruit has softened and it has reduced down to a liquid pulp
4) Strain the pulp into a clean bowl, which is best left overnight as it will take a while. If you push the pulp through you end up with a cloudy cordial and tiny fruit solids which can ferment and ruin it. The fruit pulp can be used in a crumble or apple pie so use it or freeze it for another day
5) Measure how much liquid you have in the bowl
6) Transfer the liquid into a saucepan and bring to the boil
7) Add sugar (6 to 12oz per pint of liquid) or honey (7oz per pint of liquid)
8) Simmer for a few minutes, stirring often, allowing the sugar to dissolve and the cordial thicken, avoid boiling the mixture

9) Fill the hot, sterile bottles with cordial, ensuring there is enough room for the lid, but not enough for an air gap and seal immediately, wiping the bottle clean if necessary

10) Once cool, label and store

Of course, you are unlikely to have enough cordial to exactly fill all of the bottles, and one will be partly full. In this case, do not store this part filled bottle but instead refrigerate it and use it first.

Cordial & Syrup Recipes

Here are some recipes that you can try making at home. These are great for using up excess produce and preserving the taste of summer throughout the cooler months.

Blackcurrant Cordial

This is a great recipe to make with home grown currants. Pick them when they are really dark and big, literally just before they become overripe and split.

Ingredients:

¼ pint of water per 1lb of fruit 8oz of sugar per pint of juice

Method:

1) Give the fruit a good wash and remove any stalks (if you are not planning on cooking with the left-over pulp you can leave the stalks in place)

2) Simmer the blackcurrants together with the water for between 30 and 45 minutes until the fruit has reduced to a pulp

3)   Follow the general instructions above to finish the cordial

Plum Cordial

This is another great way to use up fresh plums. Anyone with a plum tree will tell you just how many plums you end up with, so this is a nice alternative to sauce or stewing the plums. This can be

made from windfall plums, just remove any bruised bits and the stones, if you are planning on using the pulp later.

Ingredients:
¼ pint water per 1lb of fruit
12oz / 340g of sugar per pint (570ml) of plum juice

Method:
1)   Put the plums and water into a saucepan and simmer on a low to medium heat, stirring occasionally until they fall apart
2)   Mash the mixture using a potato masher or the back of a wooden spoon
3)   Follow the general instructions above to finish the cordial

Lemon & Geranium Cordial

This is an unusual cordial, but one that is very pleasant, particularly good when diluted with lemonade or even white wine.

Ingredients:
20¼ fl oz / 600ml water

6oz / 170g caster (superfine) sugar Juice from 2 lemons
Between 15 and 20 geranium leaves (lemon scented)

Method:
1) Boil the water in a saucepan
2) Add the lemon juice and sugar, stirring until dissolved

3) Remove from the heat and add the geranium leaves, covering the pan and leave for an hour to infuse
4) Taste the liquid, if it doesn't have enough flavor then reheat it and add more leaves before allowing to infuse for a further hour
5) Strain the cordial through a muslin bag, discarding the geranium leaves
6) Bottle the cordial following the instructions detailed earlier

Strawberry Syrup

A very nice syrup that is great on desserts and ice cream. Use fresh strawberries, ideally in season, for maximum taste.

Ingredients:
2.2lbs / 1kg fresh strawberries (hulled) White (granulated) sugar to taste

Method:
1) Wash the strawberries and remove any bruised parts
2) Put a heat proof bowl over a saucepan of boiling water (double boiler) and heat the fruit until the juice runs freely
3) Crush the fruit in the bowl, using a spoon or potato masher

4) Strain through a jelly bag

5) Add 12oz / 345g of sugar for every 20¼ fl oz / 600ml of juice, adjusting to compensate for the sweetness of the strawberries and your personal preference

6) Heat the juice on a low heat, adding the sugar

7) Stir until the sugar has fully dissolved and do not boil

8) Bottle following the procedure detailed earlier

Elderflower Cordial

For many people, elderflower cordial is the taste of summer and is absolutely delicious. Elderflowers are usually out in April to June, depending on where you live and this cordial is best made with freshly picked heads. It is best to leave them to stand for a while outside before using them to allow any insects to vacate the flowers.

Ingredients:

Approximately 25 elderflower heads 2.2lb / 1kg granulated (white) sugar Juice and zest of 1 orange

Juice and zest of 3 lemons 1 teaspoon citric acid

Method:

1) Place the insect free flower heads in a large bowl

2) Add the zest from both the lemons and the orange

3) Pour 1.5 litres (2½ pints) of boiling water over them

4) Cover and leave to infuse overnight
5) Strain the liquid through a jelly bag
6) Put the liquid into a saucepan with the sugar, citric acid and citrus juice
7) Heat on a low heat, stirring often, whilst the sugar dissolves
8) Simmer for a further two or three minutes
9) Bottle following the previous procedure

Apple & Blackberry Cordial

This is a great way to use up some fresh blackberries and windfall apples. It is great diluted with water or lemonade. I'd recommend soaking the blackberries in a bowl of water with a little bit of salt as this will encourage any wildlife to vacate the fruit. As always, remove any damaged or diseased fruits and you do not need to peel or core the apples.

Ingredients:
2.2lb / 1kg eating apples 17½oz / 500g blackberries
White (granulated) sugar at a ratio of 15oz / 420g sugar to 1 pint / 570ml juice
Juice of 1 lemon

Method:
1) Wash the apples, cut out any bruised parts and chop
2) Soak and tidy up the blackberries
3) Put the fruit in your preserving pan, half covering with water
4) Heat slowly, until it boils, then simmer for about 15-20 minutes until the fruit is soft and very squishy
5) Add the lemon juice, stirring well
6) Strain overnight (do not squeeze the fruit through the jelly bag)
7) Measure the fruit juice and return it to the pan
8) Add sugar at the correct ratio and heat, stirring until the sugar has completely dissolved
9) Bring to the boil then boil hard for five minutes
10) Bottle following the usual procedures

Nettle Cordial

This is a fabulous drink for the spring time and a great way to get your own back on the annoying nettles which grow in your garden. This recipe works well with fresh, young nettle tops. This cordial is best refrigerated and will last 4 to 6 weeks.

Ingredients:

2.2lb / 1kg white (granulated) sugar 7oz / 200g nettle tops (freshly picked) 1½oz / 40g citric acid
17 fl oz / 500ml water

Method:
1) Wash and dry the nettle tops (a salad spinner works well)
2) Put the water, sugar and citric acid into your preserving pan and heat to 140F / 60C, stirring until the sugar is dissolved
3) Remove from the heat, add the nettles and stir, ensuring the leaves are covered by water
4) Cover, and leave for a week to infuse, stirring daily
5) Strain through a sieve and bottle

Conclusion

Preserving fresh produce is something that has, sadly, fallen out of favor with the easy availability of fresh fruits and vegetables all year round. When produce was seasonal, it was more important to preserve it for the months when it was not available, but now it is a great way of preserving a glut of fresh produce and making the most of everything you grow at home or forage from the wild.

There are a huge number of ways to preserve food, which we have discussed in this book and innumerable recipes for doing so. The best part of preserving your own produce is that you can adjust the recipes to your personal preferences and make things you really enjoy. If you are diabetic, then you can adjust the sugar levels to make the preserved produce more suitable for you. If you don't like a specific spice, don't use it and replace it with something you do like!

Home-made produce is delicious and looks fantastic, plus, when presented nicely, can make an excellent gift for Christmas or birthdays. It will be appreciated as people understand the effort that went into growing and making the preserved product.

The first couple of preserves you make may take you a bit more time than usual as you get used to the process, but as you get to grips with preserving produce, it will become easier and easier. You will be able to adjust the recipes to your tastes and start to understand the best ways to preserve the fruits and vegetables.

Preserving your own produce does take work, but it is very rewarding as you can literally fill your shelves with fresh, stored produce, some of which will last until the following season! Most of the equipment you need you will already have in your kitchen, but there are a few items you may need to buy. These can be found locally or you can order them online.

Buying bottles and jars for preserving can be expensive, but if you are canning then you need to ensure you buy good quality jars that can withstand the canning process. For jams, pickles and many other preserves, glass jars with plastic coated lids are required. You can recycle jars you use at home and can ask friends and family to keep jars for you. Just ensure that all jars have the labels removed and are thoroughly cleaned. Depending on what was originally in the jar, there may be some residual smell or taste which you need to get rid of so it doesn't affect your preserve.

When preserving produce, the most important thing to do is ensure you label everything you make, not only with the name of the preserve, but also with the date you made it. I'd recommend also writing an expiry date on each item so that you don't need to remember how long each jar or bottle will last. This will allow you to use items with the shortest shelf life first and reduce wastage.

There is plenty of items you can preserve, and this can be done with freshly grown produce or produce from the supermarket. I will often check out the supermarkets for marked down fruit and vegetables that I can make into a preserve, usually things that I cannot grow where I live, but sometimes I'll just buy ingredients to make my favorite preserves.

Enjoy making your own preserves at home. It is great fun and the best way to make everything you have grown at home last for a long time. Whether you have a fruit tree or two, a couple of fruit bushes or a vegetable plot, you can enjoy your fresh preserves and know that you are eating something that you have made and know exactly what is in. I particularly like the fact that all of these preserves have no artificial ingredients in.

Have fun with these recipes and enjoy preserving your own produce at home. It is a wonderfully rewarding hobby and lets you enjoy delicious, home preserved food throughout the year.

Thank you for reading!

www.ingramcontent.com/pod-product-compliance
Lightning Source LLC
Chambersburg PA
CBHW071620080526
44588CB00010B/1199